THE NATURE OF CENTERED EMOTION

●

WANDA V. MORGAN

AuthorHouse™
1663 Liberty Drive
Bloomington, IN 47403
www.authorhouse.com
Phone: 1-800-839-8640

First published by AuthorHouse 4/2/2010

ISBN: 978-1-4490-8665-7 (e)
ISBN: 978-1-4490-8664-0 (sc)

Library of Congress Control Number: 2010904233

Printed in the United States of America
Bloomington, Indiana

This book is printed on acid-free paper.

Other books by this author:

"Become as a Child"
"Pictorgraphics"

* * * * To four special people: my sister Florence, whose free spirit is a delight, and my three children, Sharon, Tami, and Michael, whom God blessed me with as friends.

CONTENTS

INTRODUCTION

SECTION ONE

Psycological Orientation To Centering

UNIT A

UNIT B

SECTION TWO

As Above - So Below

UNIT A

UNIT B

UNIT C

SECTION THREE

As Within - So Without

UNIT A

UNIT B

SECTION FOUR

The Centered Self

INTRODUCTION

FREE WILL

The inate tendency of man to establish himself as a single force, fighting for survival and supremacy against all other things, is the nature of the human being. The will of man is the strength of man. He chooses his goals and his will enables him to achieve these goals.

The prime goal of mankind must be the goal of self realization. If the human being does not understand himself, he will not understand his world. This is the condition of most people today. Confusion blurs the vision, man is lost in his self constructed mental maze. He believes the world is out of focus, not adding up and making the necessary sense to provide the security he needs. The conditions of the world do not make sense within themselves, as they are separated conditions. It is up to each person, to make his own sense out of these conditions.

If the world appears distorted and pointless, remember, it is the viewer who determines what he sees.

In the same manner that people rebel against exterior things, their mental state reflects an inner battle. Each person is engaged in conflict within himself. Only when this inner battle ceases, will exterior battles cease to be a part of his experience. The world comes into order at the same instant the mind comes into order.

The logical function of the mind is to weigh, balance, and determine between two existing choices, to arrive at a final conclusion establishing a summation between two things. It is this ability of the mind that enables one to do the computing necessary to survive and advance in a material way.

When one solves a difficult mathematical problem, he experiences a centered (together) feeling of well being; an emotional rush of pleasure. This same feeling of well being is identified with success in any endeavor.

The misunderstood use of the analytical aspect of mind applied in an attempt to provide emotional gratification results in dependence on outer conditions existing in such a way as to supply self satisfaction. When outer conditions do not bring about this desired satisfaction, one believes that changing his outer conditions will solve his emotional delema, much as if he had arrived at an erroneous solution to a mathematical problem and must "search" for the correct solution. He may leave a trail of "wrong" people, "wrong" jobs, "wrong" places to live etc., behind him in his desperate seach for the "right" person, the "right" job, and the "right" place to live. He never realizes that the problem is himself, and that the answer lies within himself and cannot be found "existing" any where outside of himself.

THE DUAL EXISTANCE WITHIN

I HATE AND I LOVE.
PERHAPS YOU ASK WHY I DO SO.
I DO NOT KNOW, BUT I FEEL IT,
AND I AM IN TORMENT.
Catullus, Odes

This book deals primarily with the interaction of self with self: the conflicts experienced within the self that arise from a basic self rejection. There is only one answer to all self confusion. An integration must take place wherein one accepts all of his self aspects without reservation. When this happens, the problems that one faces in life can be met with from a standpoint of self strength gained through total self recognition and total self acceptance.

14

THE EMOTIONAL SELF

All that is emotion, lives through all that is humanity. The emotional
senses go deeper than skin color, cultures, and beliefs. The joy that
you have felt, is the joy that I have felt. The sorrow that I have known,
is the sorrow that you have known, for these things are of one.

Emotional experiences do not just happen to us. We personally create
them. An adverse emotional experience is not something apart from
one that comes and settles on the head of an otherwise peace loving person and causes him to act in a manner foreign to his nature. The unpleasant emotion is a part of the person and surfaces when something
disagrees with what he believes should be so.

When an adverse condition is allowed to cause one to lose control of
himself, he is a living breathing demonstration of that emotion, he IS
anger, hate, et cetera. The same is true of a person when he expresses
true love and compassion for a fellow human being, he IS love, he IS
compassion. The truth of this carries quite an insight into the nature of
self when fully comprehended. To know that "I am" the love of the world,
"I am" the hate of the world, is a revelation. To believe that I experience hate or love as a transient emotion is a far different thing than to
know that at the moment, I am, that thing that I express. Emotions are
not "borrowed" for temporary use. Emotions "are" the person. To
feel bitter because of any external circumstance is still to "be" a bitter
mind and body.

EXPERIENCING EMOTION

Thinking is a mechanical process of the mind. Without the interplay of
emotion that we experience with thought, we would be nothing more than
analytical computers. In order to "experience" a thing, which thought
processing in itself cannot do, we have been provided by nature, with the
ability to experience emotion.

If we were to simply scan a sunset, minus an emotional experience, the
sunset would appear to us as being a horizon line, with geometrical lines
and circles arranged about it. Our own emotions provide the "beauty"
we see.

All of life's emotional experience cannot be the peaceful experience such as when we view beautiful things. This type of emotional experience requires no effort on our part, as these experiences are given to us as a birthright. Life would be dull indeed without them. There are many self destructive emotions, however, that we could live happier, and longer, without. Each unpleasant emotion stems from a direct lack of true understanding of the self. We can learn to see "beauty" in all aspects of life through the realization that we do create our own emotional reality, even when that reality is not so pleasant. The manner in which we choose to see reality, is not a fixed immovable thing. Our adverse emotional experiences will change when we choose to "see" differently.

It is the writer's aim to convince the reader that he is the final determiner of his own self worth, as well as being in a central position of full control over all of his emotional experiences. A methodical form of repetition has evolved as a matter of necessity in bringing this message clearly home to the reader. If one example does not cause this awareness, possibly another one will.

"CENTERING"
EMOTIONS THROUGH THE USE OF:

FOUR FOLD
SIMULTANEOUS
CONTRAST

There is nothing new under the sun, but there are new ways to observe things that we have seen before. Sometimes a new approach can lead to new insights. The following hypothesis served to "pull together" many familiar concepts regarding the emotional nature of the human being into one whole configuration.

Modifying extreme opposites through the use of:

FOUR FOLD SIMULTANEOUS CONTRAST*

* The mental act of observing four oppositional reference points at the same time, rather than the usual two.

MODIFYING EMOTION

The opposite of "emotion" is commonly assumed to be "no emotion" or "minus emotion". It is assumed that to be "without emotion" would be to exist simply as a mechanical robot.

This proposition is shown as:

EMOTION

MINUS
EMOTION

Four Fold Simultaneous Contrast affords a method of subdividing pertinent points of reference in order to modify extreme divisions:

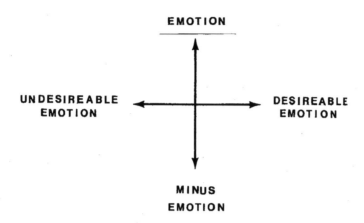

This modification brings forth possibilities of a more to be desired choice existing between these two extremes. It is not necessary to abolish all emotion in order to be free from disturbing emotion.

All of the charts used in this book are based on the simple principle of modifying extreme opposites through the use of a pertinent subdivision. In most cases the origin of this modification is immediately apparent to the reader. In other instances, the origin of the subdivision may not be obviously apparent but becomes so upon deeper reflection, if one feels the need to do so.

SUGGESTED READING TECHNIQUE

As a new concept, this introduction to Four Fold Simultaneous Contrast presents a need for an open mind to allow for new ways of thought. This is not a difficult to comprehend proposal and if the reader will bear with me, it will be seen that light, easy reading makes up the major portion of this book. Four Fold Simultaneous Contrast provides for an added dimension of comprehension to the present two point comparison system. It is used here as a basis for elaboration and subsequent clarification in particular areas of self understanding. Read lightly, do not attempt to read anything more into each page than is obvious at surface reading. If a question arises in your mind, it should resolve itself shortly as the text progresses.

SECTION ONE

psycological

orientation to:

Centering

PERSONAL ISOLATION

Each person is a single oneness representing a unique version of an universally shared consciousness. We must recognize this initial state of isolation before we will ever experience true communication with another person. This may be a frightening concept at first, for to be isolated from other people in life is the most feared state. We need to see ourselves reflected in another person's eyes to provide an inner assurance of our very existance. It is when this need of other people is misunderstood in that the image reflected in their eyes tell us who we are that the principle of "personal isolation" must be recognized as a step toward self realization. For other people do not know who we are. One can only know himself wholly.

Peace can be found within the self, not exterior at all. We have given our wholeness away to people and things to do with as they choose, simply because we did not know any better way to still the raging conflict and turmoil existing in our own minds. We demand that others still the inner storm, soothe the inner wound, through words of love and praise that make us feel whole. Others are not able to do this for us, for they exist as we do, amid the strife of inner conflict living alone among people. This is why no relationship ever really satisfies. This is why life becomes a compromise and we live the proverbial lives of quiet desperation.

Sooner or later each must face this state of aloneness if only ultimately at the time of death. There is a much more desired way of facing the alone state and that is to recognize and conquer through self knowledge that which we have feared needlessly. The final facing of one's self and finding it to be the whole self for which we have been yearning, is to be born into a new sense of self strength, the strength that may have lived a life time and never been recognized. When this is done death itself will lose its sting.

SEPARATE FROM ALL OTHER THINGS

Total security ended for each individual when expulsion from the mother's womb took place. From that time a fearful insecure state became a part of the human psyche. The search for material security has been embarked upon.

THE INSECURE SELF ATTEMPTS TO FIND SECURITY THROUGH THINGS EXTERIOR TO HIMSELF BUT CANNOT, SIMPLY BECAUSE NO SECURITY EXISTS THERE TO BE FOUND.

UNIT

A

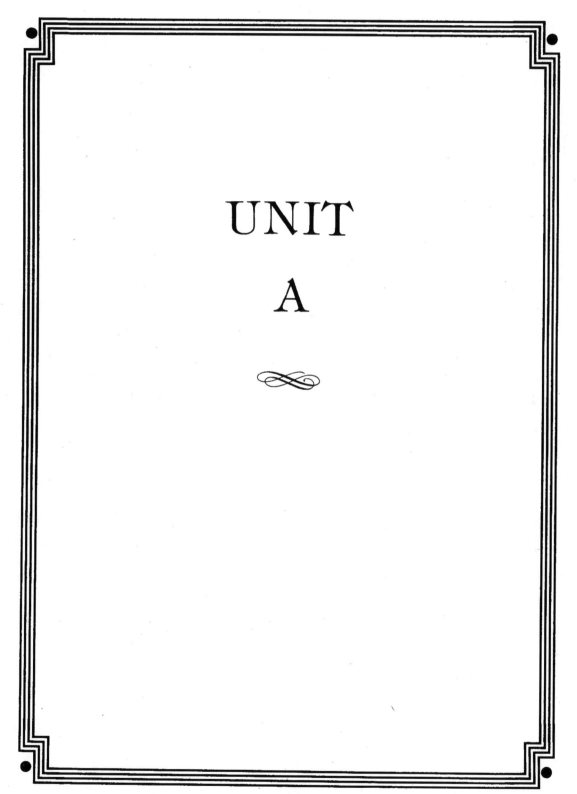

CENTER ORIENTATION

CENTER ORIENTATION

The need to be oriented in mind and body is basic to all people. Familiar surroundings provide a form of mental security even when those surroundings are not all that is hoped for.

An attempt to expand our mental orientation is expressed in the question, "What is consciousness?" This becomes a universal question that can only ask, "What is life?" In an effort to know it all, we may miss the obvious and only aspect of consciousness that contains any real applicable meaning to the individual. To each person, "consciousness" can only be a state of personal mental awareness; a central point of comprehension of one's personal reality.

TWO ASPECTS OF ORIENTATION

Our total existance is experienced through the combined aspects of being both physical (material) and mental (thought). Orientation of both aspects are experienced. Though these are two inseparable parts of one whole, the orientation is not the same. This proposal is explained in detail on the following four pages.

PHYSICAL ORIENTATION

Each individual consciousness becomes personally oriented into the material world. A conclusion, at first observation, is that this is accomplished simply through the input of the five senses; sight, sound, smell, taste, and touch. Through this concept, we are separated discerning observers, of all "things". Since our bodies consist of matter also, it is not possible that we are in the total sense separated from the like physical matter that we observe. The sensory input through way of the body (sensation) and the resulting output (reaction) provides for interaction of ourselves with other material things.

Orientation of the physical self consists of observing outside activity existing on a six point reference system. The physically oriented self contacts other matter through the five senses as well as through the analytical mind.

CENTER ORIENTATION TO:

FOUR FOLD SIMULTANEOUS CONTRAST

IMPORTANT: READ ALL CHARTS FROM "CENTER" OUT

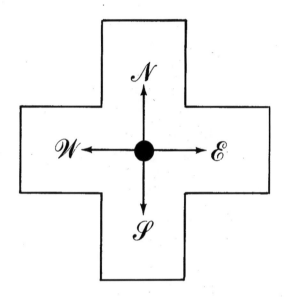

Oppositionally based structure showing:

● Centered Personal Orientation

The directional Cardinal Reference Points of the compass are a structured system devised by the human mind to gain physical and mental orientation; a method of determining the location of various landmarks that surround one.

Observation and comprehension functions are shared by all, while Central Interpretation results from unique interpretation as concluded by the individual.

PSYCOLOGICAL ORIENTATION TO MATTER

Places the mind at the "Center" observing all things that surround one Central point of awareness. The fact that worldly things are made of matter is not so conclusive as the fact that all that is matter must revolve around one central point of awareness to gain definition.

Physical and mental focalization of any one given Place and time:

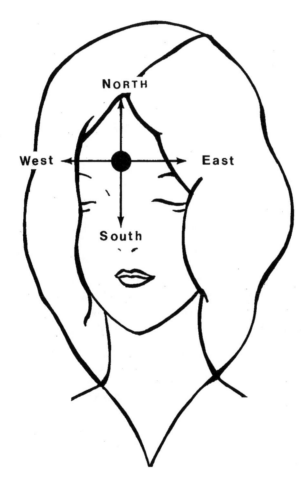

⚫ "Everything is 'somewhere' in relation to where I am"

FOUR CARDINAL REFERENCE POINTS PROVIDE

A STRUCTURED CENTER ORIENTATION TO:

MATERIAL PERSPECTIVE

FIVE SENSES

TIME AND ELEMENTS

There exists no concept of life that is not experienced as a central observer defining all things that surround one point of consciousness.

The following three charts are based on commonly acknowledged opposites descriptive of the above three categories. Each chart requires supplimental descriptives in the initial four reference areas in order to explore the full concept of each subject. These supplimentals result in a total of twelve references in each.

These charts result in a pictorial observation of a proposed "structured" system in which each person exists as a central interpretor of all things that surround him.

This is done for the purpose of integrating elusive aspects of life that may cause one to feel small, defenseless and possibly disoriented in this vast world of "things" that we live in. The world may be vast, but the particular area that one personally occupies is no larger than his own chosen mental dimensions.

MATERIAL PERSPECTIVE

MATERIAL PERSPECTIVE

Cardinal Reference Points Depicting Material Perspective

CENTERED OBSERVATION OF THE MATERIAL WORLD OF FACTUAL
REALITY

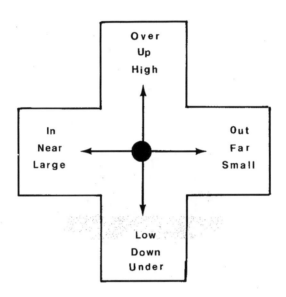

Material Perspective

The mind's function within these Cardinal Reference Points indicate an observing condition, simultaneously with a personal interpretation of what has been observed.

Because we tend to observe as solid matter, all "things" that surround us, we have arrived at the erroneous conclusion that all things that we "see", both visually and through mental comprehension, are solid indicators of "factual" conditions. This is misleading, in that a person believes that he simply observes facts, and that all facts appear the same to all people. In truth, there are very few things that are seen exactly the same way by all people.

Each person is subject to programming by structures of society. Due to the variety of accepted beliefs of various cultures, wide chasms of beliefs exist between various groups of people. Each of these groups consider their cause to be right and factual. Racial, religious, and political beliefs differ radically.

Your beliefs are primarily the product of information given to you as factual, based on the truths common to your particular culture. These beliefs were accepted as truths by you, just as the fact that the sun rises and sets was accepted as a truth. The observable rising and setting of the sun is an ABSOLUTE DETERMINER provided by nature. Beliefs are provided by human beings.

The term "having something in common with someone" indicates that you and another person have arrived at near conclusions regarding any given subject. In general each person may believe the other to be slightly mad. We may believe ourselves to be so, if we fail to find one who agrees with our particular version of reality. Groups and clubs are formed in an effort to provide emotional security for the individuals, in the form of commonly shared belief structures.

FIVE SENSES

Five Senses

CARDINAL REFERENCE POINTS OF FIVE SENSES

DEPICTING:

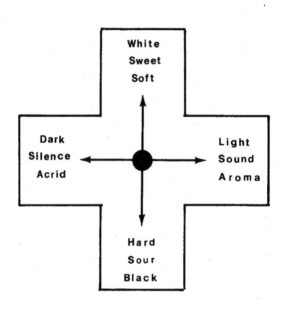

● Centered "experiential" functioning of the five senses.

FIVE SENSES DESCRIPTIVES

TASTE: SWEET - SOUR   SMELL: ACRID - AROMA

TOUCH: SOFT - HARD   HEARING: SOUND - SILENCE

SIGHT: LIGHT - DARK (BLACK - WHITE; COLORS; LIGHT RAYS)

PERSONAL SENSITIVITY COINCIDES WITH EMOTIONAL REACTIONS

In the area of the five senses, personal preferences are established. We experience subtle emotional reactions to all of what we see, hear, touch, smell, and taste. These reactions establish our personal "sense personality". We avoid the unpleasant and choose the pleasant.

PERSONAL SENSITIVITY VARIABLES:

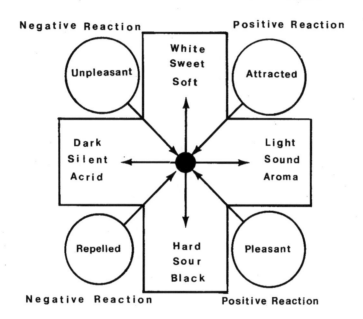

Negative Reaction   Positive Reaction

Unpleasant   White Sweet Soft   Attracted

Dark Silent Acrid   Light Sound Aroma

Repelled   Hard Sour Black   Pleasant

Negative Reaction   Positive Reaction

● Sense Personality

The existing cardinal reference points have no positive-negative content of themselves, but gain these definitions through personal choices.

Physical comfort is experienced through the choices existing to the senses. This is one area where we "know" what would please us. Since these "sense" things are often unatainable, we mistakenly become convinced that the acquisition of these things would bring us the happiness and peace of mind that we long for. This is not so, but rare is the person who knows it.

TIME AND ELEMENTS

TIME AND ELEMENTS

CARDINAL REFERENCE POINTS DEPICTING SEASONAL ELEMENTS
SUGGESTING UNDERLYING TIME STRUCTURE

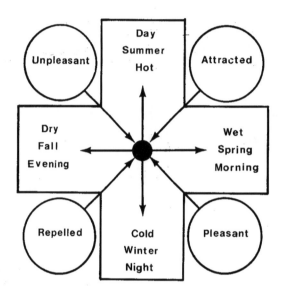

● **Personal Environmental Preferences**

STRUCTURED TIME AND SPACE

The material world is built on structure. Time is one of the most obvious structures used by man. We need this time structure to bring order to our lives and to give us a feeling of security in the vastness of eternity; "I am here, now, and I will be there, tomorrow", provides me with the assurance that I know where "I am" in relation to time. It allows for references to the past, present, and future, in terms that all can comprehend.

We also rely on structure to provide space orientation. We orient our-selves in space, logically, physically, and emotionally. Hell is down, heaven is up. We need "elbow" room, and a special space that is our own. We divide space into rooms, towns, cities, states, and countrys.

We look to the heavens for further orientation when we have satisfact-orily determined our "position" in space. One can then knowledgeably make this factual statement: "I am standing on solid ground, contained within inner space, on the earth's surface, in the United States of Amer-ica, in the state of California, in the County of Santa Clara, in the City of San Jose, on Main Street." I can now feel secure in the knowledge of where "I am" in relation to the vastness of all space. This mental or-ientation allows me to relax within the structure of my personal space reference.

The desire to find what outer space consists of, is inate in human minds. This desire comes from a basic drive to further orient ourselves and provide more space "reference". Science works toward conquering out-er space as a material practical goal, the human soul is searching for something more. Science will gradually explore and explain further to mankind what is contained in outer space areas, however, exploration of space will never lead to the discovery of heaven, for heaven and hell are aspects of one's own mind.

HOW WE PERCEIVE TIME AND SPACE

We stand in awe of these areas because we are not aware of the total self that we are. We believe that somewhere, in that vast unexplainable area of undiscovered time and space, the answer to life lies obscured from our lowly perception. We have not accepted the fact, that the only "real" time is now, and the only "real" space is that which we ourselves, person-ally, occupy. The answers to life, that we search for, lie within our selves, in our "now" time, not lost without in an impersonal meaningless eternity.

Our concepts of time and space are a result of a structuring system that has evolved from drawing the obvious conclusions in these areas. When suggestions are made of the possibilities that defy these man made rules, the usual reaction is amazement and incredulity. An effort to provide in-stant orientation often leads one to draw premature conclusions.

EMOTIONALLY INFLUENCED LOGIC

CENTER ORIENTATION TO LOGIC

FOUR CARDINAL REFERENCE POINTS - MATHEMATICALLY BASED ABSOLUTE DETERMINERS

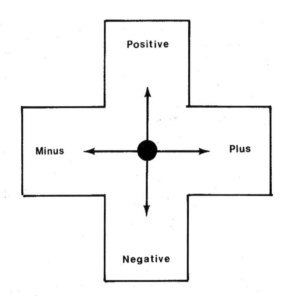

● Logical Analysis

Pure logical thought minus emotional content is rare, and the difference is an important point to be made. What we believe to be logical reasoning, in many cases actually contain our own emotional reactions, so that one person's logic may be another person's illogic. In order to execute pure logical reasoning we must use ABSOLUTE DETERMINERS, that is, a base concept that means the same to all people. Mathematics are a reliable source of a universally accepted absolute determiner. This may be the only reliable source.

EMOTIONALLY INFLUENCED LOGIC

SENSITIVITY VARIABLES INJECT EMOTIONAL INFLUENCE:

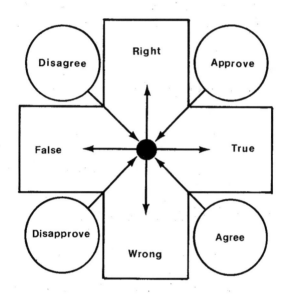

● **Emotionally Influenced Logic**

The Cardinal Reference Points: Right-Wrong, True-False, are not absolute determiners and depend on personal interpretations which are influenced by personal emotional reactions.

"ONE MAN'S SENSE IS ANOTHER MAN'S NONSENSE"*

* Author Unknown

EMOTIONALLY INFLUENCED LOGIC

The use of languages of the various cultures, are common absolute determiners, only in that we are able to read and write our thoughts, and the thoughts of others, thereby establishing a concrete method of communication. These communications are not absolute determiners any more than speach is, as the spoken word is subject to individual interpretation. This is where pure logic is lost, and personal interpretation takes over. The choices of each person, represent the absolute determiners of his factual truths. He believes he is using pure logic to arrive at his conclusions, but is actually emotionally influenced in his perception.

When the act of "comparing" causes inner distress, one has stopped using logical reason, and has entered into an emotionally self destructive method of evaluation.

PERSONAL VIEWPOINT:

The order brought to one's personal version of reality, occurs through the reasoning powers of his own mind.

OUTER CONDITIONS EXIST:

Your personal reality, is your personal interpretation of outer conditions.

YOU CREATE YOUR PERSONAL REALITY:

You are doing so now, as you read these words and interpret them to mean what you want them to mean. Your total personal reality is experienced in the world of your mind. There exists no one valid reality as experienced by all people.

Each person, personally creates his version of the world, as well as his personal emotional experiences within his world. The full acceptance of this one fact, will cause each person who is aware of his true position of self control, will "take" control.

UNIT

B

OPPOSITIONALLY BASED

EMOTIONAL STRUCTURES

OPPOSITIONALLY BASED EMOTIONAL STRUCTURE

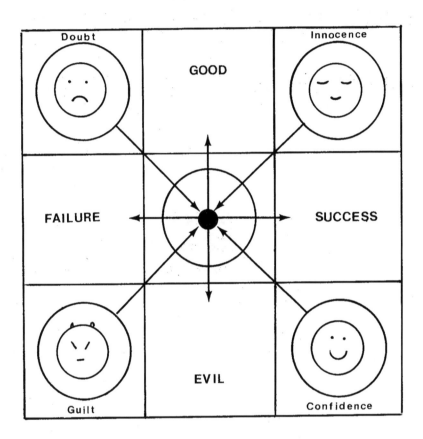

This "Master" structure will serve to familiarize the reader with the basic emotional relationships used in this book. Uncomplicated and containing a trace of humor in the illustrations depicting the basic emotional "faces", this thesis never the less conveys a much needed insight into the emotional nature of the human being.

SOCIETY'S STRUCTURES

INITIAL OPPOSITES

There is no way one can explore the subject of emotion without beginning with the concepts of Good versus Evil. To a religious person, God is synonymous with "good" and Satan is synonymous with "evil". If one is not religiously inclined, he simply thinks of these opposites as "Society's" "good and "evil". These opposites will be referred to as the latter, for the purpose of this book, which is more inclined to be an analysis.

MODIFIERS:

The structures of Society's Good and Evil are subdivided by the modifiers "Success" and "Failure", as Good versus Evil are impersonal references until one feels his personal experiences influenced by these structures of society.

FOUR PRIMARY EMOTIONS:

INITIAL OPPOSITES

Personal feelings of Innocence and Guilt are products of society's evaluations of Good and Evil. These divisions are modified by the resulting feelings of Self Confidence and Self Doubt. These four primary emotions operate in a directly opposing manner which causes the major divisions within self and the resulting conflicts.

THE CENTER

●

Symbolizes self identification. First as a central observer of the principle structures of society, and secondly, as an active participant as you observe your own social interactions within this structure. This central position affords you the opportunity to observe these four common separations of self and the resulting emotional traumas.

PERSONAL

BELIEF STRUCTURES

PERSONAL BELIEF STRUCTURES

Depending upon the cultures one is exposed to as a child, each person has built a set of values that he lives by. These are actually, in every sense of the word, belief structures, as these beliefs are his life time references as to what constitutes his personal reality. These values he lives by and expects others to recognize them as he does. When people of other cultures do not recognize these particular values, his natural reaction is to defend his beliefs because they represent his reality.

Personal opinions regarding what is morally right or wrong, or what constitutes a successful society are simply personal opinions. We personally reject or accept our self truths. Our centered position on the chart at this point comes from our personal beliefs and each person believes he is standing on a rock of true knowledge. Violent inner reaction is aroused when one insists on his personal interpretation of one order and one order only. Each person feels that he knows all the answers. He will fight for the preservation of his ordered beliefs, for they are his personal ground between the opposites. He feels he cannot afford to relinquish these beliefs as they tell him who he is, they represent his personal existance and validity.

CARDINAL REFERENCE POINTS DEPICTING CENTERED ORIENTATION

TO BASIC STRUCTURES OF SOCIETY

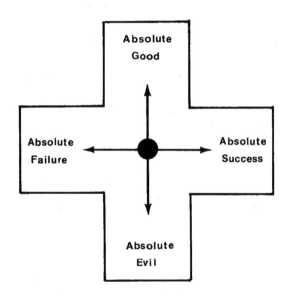

● **Personal Belief Structures**

The terms; Good versus Evil, Success versus Failure, defy universal definition. These aspects of life are subject to personal definition.

ORIENTATION TO SOCIETY'S STRUCTURES

ORIENTATION TO SOCIETY'S STRUCTURES

The following definitions are taken from Webster's Unabridged Dictionary.

HOLY	**UNHOLY**
Spiritual	Human
Angelic	Worldly
Devoted to God	Earthy
Pure in heart	Profane

Society's refinements do not encourage one to feel worthy. We are told that to be human is to be unholy, evil, profane, etc. This is done, supposedly, to instil conscience into the human mind. It seems that conscience is a natural instinctive aspect of the nature of humanity, and that what society does in fact, is to instil the terms of right and wrong as these things are judged by society. One would not be a totally evil creature as a matter of nature if one was not exposed to the sophisticated rules of society. Love and kindness are instinctive in the human emotional makeup, as well as the human traits of cruelty. We observe these traits existing in animals, surely we are no less endowed.

While society's definition of "good" brings about a form of discipline, the price is high. It also brings about a state of self rejection in each human being. While one is caught up in feelings of self rejection, he is not likely to perform in a way that brings ultimate good to himself or to his fellow citizens.

ORIENTATION TO SOCIETY'S CONCEPTS OF SUCCESS AND FAILURE

The following definitions are taken from Webster's Unabridged Dictionary.

SUCCESS	**FAILURE**
Achievement	Disaster
Triumph	Collapse
Advancement	Deterioration
Ascendancy	Derelection

The emotional "highs" and "lows" experienced during life's failures and successes allow for more trauma than is biologically health inducing.

We have too much to gain from success, and too much to lose from failure. The way failure is defined leaves no room to lose. If we lose we have lost self respect. Even the best loser, loses a part of himself with each personal failure, if he submits to external pressures from society's evaluation system.

COMPARISON AND EVALUATION

Grading is O.K. for eggs but is psychologically damaging to people.

GRADE A   GRADE B   REJECT

Self doubt is instilled in each child during his early educational years. His intelligence is measured and posted for all to observe. His athletic abilities are tested and applauded or dismissed.

A sense of self worth was arrived at during orientation to a society based on comparison, and subsequent evaluation. The winner is idolized and the failure is ridiculed. The desire to win to prove oneself worthy, has become a set part of the individual. He has thoroughly learned the art of self doubt.

Society's evaluation system will not change, we can only change from the inside; promote inner flexibility in the face of society, for we will find no flexibility outside ourselves.

SELF IMAGE

One casts the mold of his self image through impressions as received by the mind and senses (emotional sensitivity) from outside influences during the formative years of life. It is important, nevertheless, to remember that individuals will respond in as many different ways to identical treatment as there are individuals. The situation that one is born into, does not necessarily determine individual emotional experience within that situation. Personal circumstances that surround one, has an indirect influence only upon the final molded self as accepted by one's self. For even then the final choice was self willed. In the instance where an alcoholic parent is a part of the forming period, the child may have chosen to drink as his parent did, or he may have chosen to be a teetotaler, or any given degree between these two extremes.

Statements such as, "My mother or father was too strict, causing me to be so and so", or "My mother or father was too lienient, causing me to be such and such", are excuses for avoiding self responsibility. Looking into the past to find reasons why one is presently unhappy, is looking in the wrong place. It is not logical thinking, but emotional confusion, when one places blame on anyone or anything for one's present unhappiness. It is believed by some people that if they can bring to conscious awareness particular traumatic childhood incidents, this conscious knowledge would serve to resolve present emotional discomforts. It is a limitation, always, to look in the past for causes. If one is looking for peace he will not find it on a battlefield. Childhood experiences are a necessary fundamental foundation to the building of an adult who will eventually set about determining his own feeling of self worth, and the ultimate peace of mind that comes with this discovery. This self approval will come from within and others have nothing to do with it. Blaming parents for imagined or justified wrong doing during one's childhood is a waste of time, and can only serve to avoid turning to the self to find the way.

FOUR "FACES" OF

EMOTIONAL SENSITIVITY

FOUR "FACES"
OF EMOTIONAL SENSITIVITY

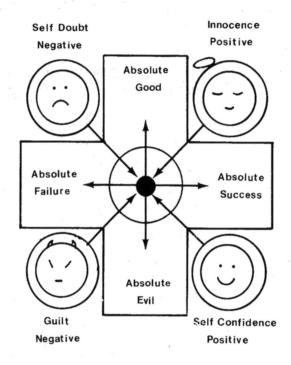

Personal experiences of:

Innocence vs Guilt   Confidence vs Doubt

A false image of self (symbolized by the circle surrounding the Center) came to be as a result of self judgment during orientation. The circle symbolizing the false self image will be shown on this chart only as the Center carries within it knowledge of all self aspects.

SELF ACCEPTANCE

As a direct result of the presently constructed rules of society which are based on comparison, competition, reward and punishment, all children are subject to warping of the natural spirit of self acceptance they are born with.

It would not occur to a child that he is in any way unacceptable if he had not been made to feel that he is not. In the process of adjusting to the material world there is an unlimited number of "should" and "should nots". Many of these rules are necessary to the preservation of an orderly society. It is the manner in which they are instilled in the child that is most damaging to the natural spirit. Most parents are untrained as to the methods best suited for this accomplishment due to the fact that each person tends to adhere to, and so perpetuate, the methods of child rearing that he himself was exposed to. Change can only come through self examination and self discovery. When one learns to accept himself, he will teach his offspring the same self acceptance methods.

 RETREAT TO THE SHELL

Spontaneous action is a natural expression of self. Spontaneity is the spiritual self in joyful life action. It expects approval and feels free to be its natural self. When disapproval is experienced, the spontaneous self quickly retreats into a shell and feels chastised. During the forming years this happens frequently. This psychological shell provides temporary respite for the tender self image as it enables the person to shut out anything it cannot cope with. These incidents can range from momentary periods of "hurt silence" to actual permanent regression in which the person refuses to communicate with others and lives totally in a fantasy world of his own making. The habit of returning to the protection of the shell is established in childhood and is carried over into adulthood to be reverted to in accordance with the varying needs of the individual. The basic need to have time to oneself is related to the shell concept that provides respite from the stresses of the outside world.

The need to erect the shell is the first hard fact of life that the self image is confronted with. People are not always kind to one another. It does not matter if the intent to hurt was really there or if the hurt was self imagined, the result sets the same retreat into action and a habit pattern is forming that ultimately causes the self image to dampen its natural aspect of spontaneity and conform to the standards preset by others as approved of behaviour.

APPROVAL

Need of approval from others during the adult life is born of self disapproval learned in childhood. Each person searches for someone who will accept, love, and approve of him as he is, in order to feel whole. Until one has experienced self integration, this search is destined to fail for one cannot expect another to love that which he does not love himself.

CONFLICTING
SELF IMAGE

CONFLICTING SELF IMAGE

During the course of orientation the mind selects and discards available input, which is personally classified as either self supportive or self deprecating, from society regarding one's self position. Ultimately, each person selects the emotionally charged ingredients that serve the purpose of self identification.

This conflicting self image remains. One is not consciously aware of this division within himself. Each exposure to outside influence results in either self image reinforcement, or in diminshed self esteem. Impressions may come directly in the form of actual demonstration from another, or merely occur in the mind's eye of the self; as you may be the recipient of actual verbal abuse or verbal compliment from another, or you may simply interpret what is occuring to mean either of these regardless of the intent.

The reason one accepts input from others as valid, is because a part of you believes what is said of you. It is not possible to comprehend that which you have not conceived of in your own mind.

If it is implied that you are unworthy in any manner, and you respond with any adverse emotional reaction, it is because you have considered yourself unworthy. The self image reflections that result during interaction with others, result from one's vulnerability to outside opinion. This is equivalent to handing one's emotions over to almost anyone at all to do with as they please.

When one is unaware of his vulnerability to suggestion, he is easy prey for unscrupulous persons who easily manipulate others into doing their bidding, through the employment of false flattery, or by instilling self doubt into his adversary.

AUTOMATIC RESPONSES

AUTOMATIC RESPONSES

Most disagreeable emotional experiences in life are a result of reacting to outer stimulus in an automatic response manner.

Nature's automatic response is necessary to avoid physical injury, and also to provide for instantaneous analytical aspects of thought, however, emotional reactions should never be allowed to operate as automatic responses. When this is done, one no longer has active control over his own emotional experiences.

Center Open To Suggestion - Automatic Responses:

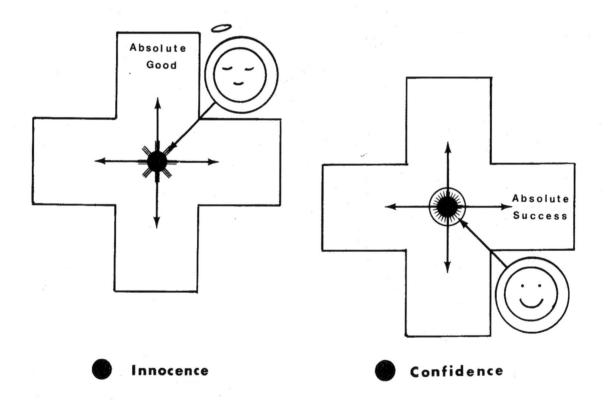

Innocence   **Confidence**

OUTSIDE APPROVAL TRIGGERS SELF ACCEPTANCE RESPONSES

OUTSIDE DISAPPROVAL TRIGGERS SELF REJECTION RESPONSES:

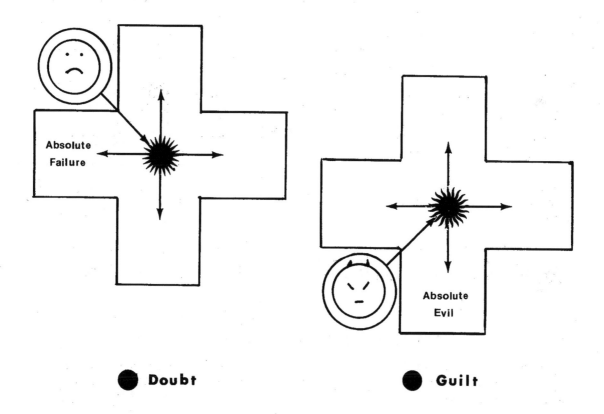

Doubt

Guilt

To have control over one's emotions means to REMAIN CALM and clear minded in all situations. The present method of "getting control" implies corrections after "loss" of control. All that one can do in order to do this is to push down and bury the anger, etc.

Another person has no more power to influence the way you view yourself than you "give" to him.

SELF LOVE - SELF HATE TRANSFERRED

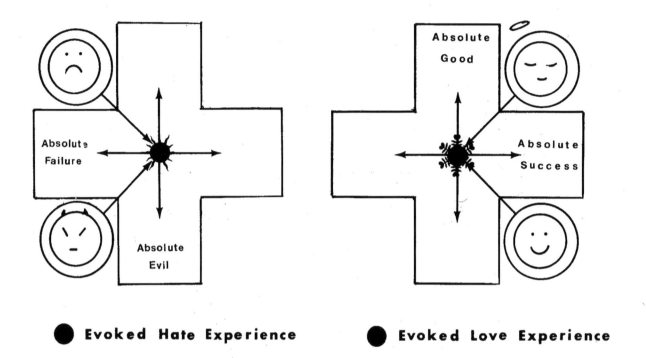

● Evoked Hate Experience   **● Evoked Love Experience**

LOVE AND HATE ARE TWO SIDES OF THE SAME COIN*

This emotional response principle can easily be tested by observing one's feelings toward a loved one who violates the unspoken "mutual consideration" agreement.

The song entitled, "Someday you'll want me to want you, and then I won't want you", is a desire for revenge, not a declaration of undying love. It is strange that we sing a "love" song with lyrics suggestive of revenge.

Other people are for companionship: not props. Romanticising of the human relationship encourages self weakness. "I need you", should be changed for: "I enjoy you". We have brainwashed ourselves to believe that our self strength rests with another person. Insistance that another love, provide emotional support, and give us a reason for living, is an aspect of human nature that we supposedly rose above through "love",

Who love too much - hate in like extreme.
Homer, Odysey

72

an unselfishness that places another person first.

In view of this human trait of dependency on other people, it may seem that if one desires the love of a particular person, that this love would be forthcoming simply through the act of "giving approval". While this may work to some extent, it must be remembered that each person controls his own reality. Another may be flattered by your attention, but not wish to follow through with the relationship that you may have in mind. If a suitor persists when he has not been accepted as such, anger or disgust can be evoked in the person being persued, as his privacy, and personal rights are being infringed upon. As for the rejected suitor, he is experiencing "self love" in its weakest form, and often turns his anger at being rejected out onto the world as he avenges his damaged self image.

Our mental "salvation" or "damnation",
does not rest in the words and deeds of
others: but in the "minds" of ourselves.

All "hate" experience is subject to the automatic response principle. We are not born hating, but learn to hate anything that appears to threaten us. We are born with the natural inclination to love, however. The trusting, smiling nature of the infant tells us this. This "natural" love becomes psuedo love, when automatic responses are allowed to rule one's emotions. "Natural" love is not subject to outer conditions but just "is". In order to return to this state of natural love, it is necessary to recognize that there are two kinds of love: one that is the opposite of hate, and one that surmounts all self conflict. It is possible to love all people. A form of all encompassing love and compassion for one's self and others becomes a part of one's psyche when he sees through the fallacies of the oppositionally based emotional experience.

One must be willing to allow many of his beliefs to dissolve in order to open his mind to new ways to "see". This is not an easy thing to do, and it will be done only when one comes to the point in his life when the old beliefs no longer serve him. If the reader has reached this plateau, he is ready to search beyond the obvious answers. There are no set rules for anyone to follow in search for his own happiness. This book is intended to provide "food for thought" that may awaken personal insights into your own unique nature.

SECTION TWO

As Above

✳

So Below

SELF CHOSEN

We are born with a mind that carries within it the spirit of God (life essence). Other than that, the mind is like a clean slate, ready to be
written on in such a way as we personally choose. We have, ourselves,
put everything that causes our unhappiness into our subconscious minds.

This particular area of the subconscious mind is actually an area of dim
awareness. It is not obscured from our vision entirely, as this area of
the mind has taken explicit orders from the conscious mind. We have
programmed ourselves to believe every concept of life that we personally
hold to be true.

Rather than look for answers to life in areas that are obscured from our
clear vision, such as life after death, previous lives, reincarnation, etc.,
we can look for applicable answers to daily problems where we will find
them, in the NOW time that we presently occupy. The desire for further
orientation leads us to speculate on these "psychic" areas of the mind,
the misconception is that this speculation holds answers for the problems
encountered in daily living.

UNIT

A

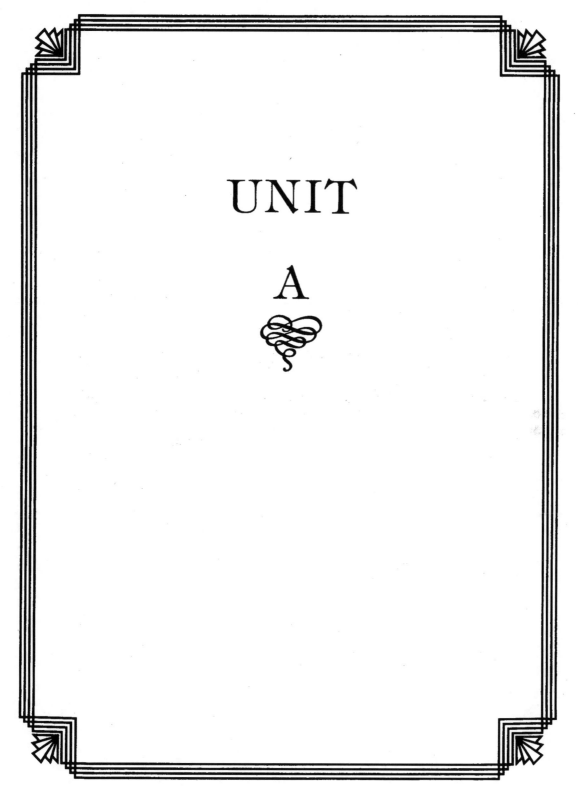

MAN'S TASK IS TO BECOME CONSCIOUS OF THE CONTENTS THAT PRESS UPWARD FROM THE UNCONSCIOUS...

IT MAY EVEN BE ASSUMED THAT JUST AS THE UNCONSCIOUS AFFECTS US, INCREASE IN OUR CONSCIOUS LIKEWISE AFFECTS THE UNCONSCIOUS.

DR. CARL JUNG

FOUR PROPOSED STATES

OF CONSCIOUSNESS

FOUR PROPOSED STATES OF CONSCIOUSNESS

The total aspect of consciousness defies explicit allocation. A clearer comprehension however, can be gained when we subtract what we know from what we do not know.

ANALYSIS OF FOUR PROPOSED STATES OF CONSCIOUSNESS
COMPOSED OF TWO INCLUSIVE OPPOSITES:

Surface As Opposed To Sub-Surface:

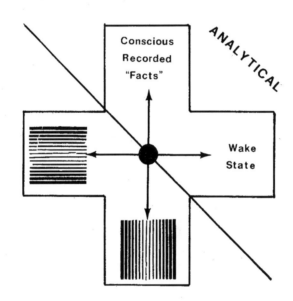

● **Surface Consciousness**

The proposed Surface Consciousness is subjunctive with the Wakeful outward focusing state of mind. Both of the propositions indicate ANALYTICAL mental activity, such as formal education, etc.

The proposed Sub-Surface Repository as referred to here, is that area of mind that we have surpressed all of the unpleasant aspects of ourselves that we could not bear to admit to consciously. The origin of these aspects can be viewed from a conscious level, which is all that is necessary to begin to disolve the repressed residule that spells unhappiness to the person who carries them written in his subconscious.

The proposed Sub-Surface Repository, is subjunctive with the Sleep State. One third of one's life is experienced in this undefined realm of consciousness that comes to us as dreams, in an on going mental activity minus conscious control. Both of these states: Sleep and Sub-Surface Repository, indicate areas of SUBLIMINAL mental activity.

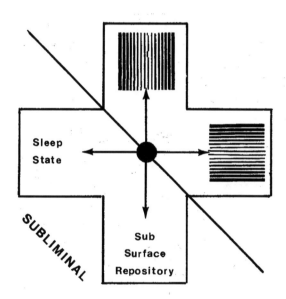

Sub-Surface Consciousness

The dream state is a combining of the conscious and subconscious mental activity. There are no laws of physics in the dream state and we may experience flying with no visible means of air support, and yet we do not question this phenomena while dreaming. This suggests that conscious controls are released for mental rest purposes, as the rigid restrictions of the laws of a material world places extreme stresses on the mind. (Many solutions to problems are revealed to one through dreams, as the mind

is free to utilize propositions that we might reject in the wake state).
It has been verified that REM (rapid eye movement), indicating a dreaming period, is required during the sleep cycle, in order to become fully
refreshed both physically and mentally. As the physical body must rest,
so must the analytical mind. It has been suggested that this release
factor may be favorable for providing clues as to specific subconscious
activity that may prove helpful to further self understanding. These "messages", however, cannot always be correctly interpreted or implicitly re-
lied upon, for as we fantasise in the wake state, this is also true of the
dream state. This is not to imply that we do not become consciously a-
ware of pertinent subconscious activity through dream interpretation, but
only that this is not the most reliable source of self insight. Reyling on
the fully conscious state of mind is far superior, for in this state we have
access to better comprehension through conscious mental analyzation.

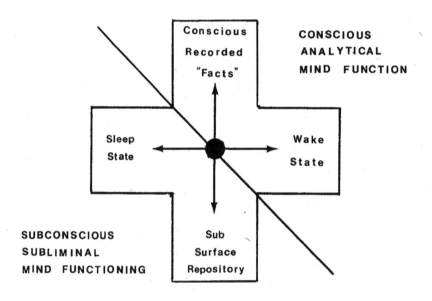

Center Of Consciousness

Each of these proposed areas of consciousness influence the other. Our
wakeful state influences our dream state as we carry conscious memory
of ourselves and circumstances into the dream state. Also, a vivid but
perhaps forgotten dream influences our wakeful state, as it has been a
part of our mental experience.

THE
NOW
EXPERIENCE

_ *Now* _

If all of your yesterdays, were gathered into bouquets
of memories,
And all of your tomorrows, shining with untold glory,
Were to fill all of "space eternal", they could not
together,
Hold the fragrance, or add the light of one small candle,
To the only time you will ever really know, the moment
that is now.

THE "NOW" EXPERIENCE

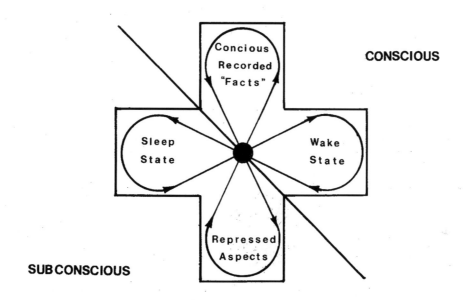

CONSCIOUS

SUBCONSCIOUS

● **"NOW" Center Focus Of Awareness**
(Present State Of Being)

The central "NOW" experience is the culmination of consciousness. One
central focus of awareness. Mental activity flows in an infinite cycle.

"AT ANY GIVEN MOMENT IN TIME A MAN IS A TOTAL STATEMENT
OF HIS BEING"*

*Author Unknown

THE EMOTIONAL CYCLE

MATHEMATICS IN MOTION

Heartbeat of the universe:

The rhythm in walking, The rhythm in talking,
The horse's gait, The flow of the tides.
The hum of a motor, The tick of a clock,
The clapping of hands, The dancing feet.
The rhymic beat· OF LIFE.

The Cyclic Symphony Of Emotional Consciousness

Much of the terminology used to describe musical composition apply as
well to the emotional sensitivities of the human being. While the structure
that underlies emotion has much in common with the underlying structures
of nature and its many evolvements, such as mathematics, the emotions
are more closely related with the phenomena of musical composition.

The Major Mode of music is descriptive of gay, happy music. The
Minor Mode is a sad, melancholy, plaintive state which is absorbed by
the emotional self as one "matches" this minor sound with his minor
"mood". It is through this minor emotional mood that one interprets the
musical inferences of the Minor Modes of music. These combined musical tones of the Major and Minor Modes are not of themselves happy or
sad, they become so through our emotional interpretations.

Music is a form of "audio" emotion. One can hear (sense) how the com-
poser "felt". Music also carries the ability to recall emotional experience to a finite degree. One can hear (sense) his emotions being replayed
after any number of years. An old man is young again upon hearing a song
of his youthful years. This is not simply a reminder of one's youth, but is
actually a form of transposition of self. Webster's definition of transpose;
to "alter in form; to transform [Obs.] The "moods" set by musical ar-
rangements that accompany motion pictures, stage plays, etc., are care-
fully contrived to evoke particular emotional reactions from the audience.
This "mood" music does more to convince the viewer of the reality of the
plot than do the actors. The accompanying music causes one to "project"
himself into the proper mood as desired by the musical arranger.

MUSICAL TONES ARE TO THE EMOTIONS WHAT MATHEMATICS ARE TO THE
ANALYTICAL MIND.

88

EMOTIONAL PRESENT STATE OF BEING

By following the arrows in the chart below, it can be seen that each emotional "zone" leads directly to its opposite. As the Center is encountered the system is channeled to include all four primary zones of emotion. One never experiences a "single" emotion, as all that one is, is experienced as a "Central Focus" of emotion, so that each of your emotional experiences include your underlying self concepts in all aspects of life.

POSITIVE EMOTIONAL EXPERIENCE

Elation Zone

MAJOR MODE

N   P

NEGATIVE EMOTIONAL EXPERIENCE

P   P

Sad Zone   Zone Happy

POSITIVE EMOTIONAL EXPERIENCE

N   N

MINOR MODE

N   R

Depression Zone

NEGATIVE EMOTIONAL EXPERIENCE

● FOCUS - Of Emotional Experience

The emotional "system" is not a regulated structure that follows as a matter of course from one zone to another. While this system exhibits a constant underlying structure based on positive-negative interaction, the emotions experienced at any given time, are the emotions that one generates for himself.

CARDINAL REFERENCE POINTS OF

THE EMOTIONAL CYCLE

All emotional experience is dependent upon Positive-Negative interaction.

The major divisions between Elation and Depression establish two extreme poles of reference. Each of these initial oppositional poles include sub-divisions; Elation is sub-divided by its Modulator: Happy. Depression is sub-divided by its Modulator: Sad.

Happy-Sad opposites are extreme poles of reference in themselves and so the Cardinal References of the emotional cycle are established.

The two sets of inclusive opposites, composed of the oppositional references and their corresponding modulators, sharply divide the emotional system into the Major (UP) Mode and the Minor (DOWN) Mode.

Positive: Elation	Negative: Depression

Elation indicates an UP emotional experience. This is viewed loosely as a Positive emotional experience. While it is considered good to be emotionally UP, elation is an extreme diviation from the "even keel" that is conducive to physical and mental health. Nature provides for relief of tensions resulting from sustained elation in the form of a possible downward swing of emotion aimed toward balance. While balance exists as a potential of the Center, the ability to "focus" on what one will determines the emotional experience. This "choice" factor can cause one to be aware of his inate ability to bring himself back into balance through deliberate directed emotional control. If one is unaware of his position of Central control, he may allow the normal decline from elation to depression to become acute depression.

As each person is a product of his own particular interpretive experiences, his achieved emotional "Center" balance is somewhat different from that of all other people. Each person is considered "normal" to the extent that he does not deviate widely from accepted, approved of behavior. While this is not meant to be a discussion of mental illness of any kind, the loss of a central, acceptable "focus" of emotion leads to various classifications of mental illnesses. While some forms of mental illness are a result of physical causes, the remainder are the product of a lack of awareness in an individual that he has the "potential" to control his emotional experiences and has allowed exterior conditions to "drive him mad".

Positive: Happy   **Negative: Sad**

Exercise of Central control leads one emotionally to the more balanced condition of "Happy" - "Sad", oppositional qualities, as these opposites are indicative of lesser degrees of emotional extreme.

Happiness is most usually expressed through activity rather than verbalization. Being happy, promotes one to be filled with energy as he "acts" out his happiness in helping himself and others.

"I'm so happy, I could cry", is indicative of the intricately inherent opposition contained within the emotional experience.

When one is sad, he expresses this emotion verbally if he has anyone to listen to him. If he does not, his "sadness" may become "depression". It is not necessary to allow the fact that one is alone to determine his emotional experience, as long as he remembers his center potential to determine his own chosen emotional experience in spite of exterior situations. Awareness of the inate balance that exists in the emotional system will cause one to become aware that he need not remain sad for long and will heed the inner promptings to take action to do the things that will dissolve the unhappiness that he has "focused" upon.

It has been suggested that each person is subject to various emotional "time" cycles which are a determining factor upon his emotional experiences. Particular ages, such as puberty, change of life and so forth, produce favorable climates for particular emotional experiences. Additional tension and anxiety is sometimes experienced during the full moon which exerts an intense pulling effect on the tides and the earths surface. Since the human body is composed of water and matter also, we are not exempt from this force of nature.

While exterior things have an influence on us, we are still, through the mental power that we are, able to choose the emotions that we experience. In order to do this we must acknowledge that the major portion of our unhappiness is "self created" through direct lack of understanding of our own emotional makeup.

The purpose of this section based on the proposed aspects of consciousness and the resulting emotional system is to aid one in "integrating" his concept of consciousness in order to prompt a feeling of self control over his emotional experiences. The closer to feeling "centered" between these four emotional fluctuations, the more one will enjoy life. Emotions are a part of us, as our ability to experience emotion provides our personal illumination of reality. We can view the emotional system from a position of control, however, and learn to live in harmony within ourselves through this knowledge.

Happiness is a resultant of the relative strengths of positive and negative feelings rather than an absolute amount of one or the other.*

UNIT

B

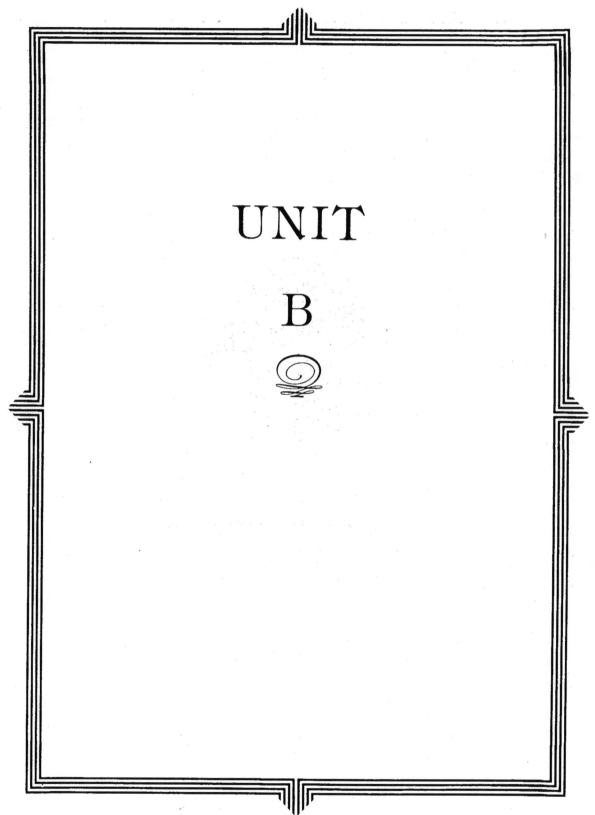

THE FIFTH STATE OF

CONSCIOUSNESS

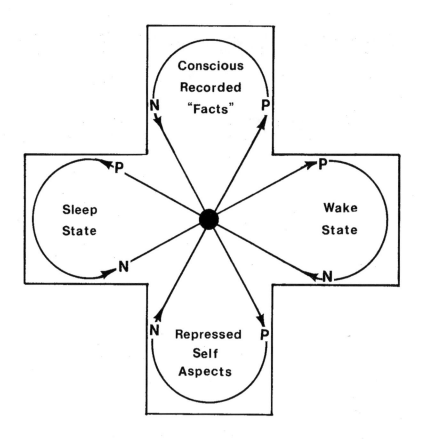

Fifth State Of Consciousness

The creative ability of the mind to focus, aspire, determine, etc., are an integral part of the NOW Center of Awareness. Here we dare to be different. This NOW Center of Awareness is concurrent with our own free will, as well as, our mental connection with all things

FIFTH STATE OF CONSCIOUSNESS

Instinct and intuition are provided to us through the NOW Center, for while the NOW Center is the focal point of conscious awareness it also comes to us from all that is. It is the Essence of life. This inward nature of the human, underlying one's material manifestations (beliefs) is one's true substance. The NOW Center is a well spring from which we may draw newness.

The entire contents of this book, of course, is directed to the Fifth State of Consciousness, which is your natural (nature-all) centered condition. You have been there all along and perhaps did not know it, for to be centered in self is a necessary stablized state that each person knows. From the time you realized that you were separate from all other things you began your center orientation. There are many distractions existing in the oppositional nature of mankind that draws him away from conscious awareness of his natural centered condition, however, each has succeeded in attaining a balance between the opposites as is reflected in each persons unique personality.

If we did not have choices, we would all be the very same, and this choice factor that we have been given (free will) is what separates us from all other forms of life and gives dominion to the human being over all other things. This dominion and self determining mind, serves a far deeper purpose than to merely rule over the birds and beasts of the earth. It has been provided so that mankind has the inner mental ability to raise his consciousness; to bring about a full awareness of what life is, into the minds of living beings. For all of our uniqueness, we share in this search for a meaning to life, and we all have been provided with the "Centered" state from which to draw newness.

"CENTERED" CHOICE

As one has consciously believed (past) so he subconsciously believes (present). We have programmed our minds to believe that opposition to each and every desire is valid. Each resolution for self betterment is thought to be destined to give way in the face of the contrary "opposing self" or at the very least a tremendous inner battle must be undergone before the newly accepted thought patterns regarding self are established.

Efforts to diet, quit smoking etc., respond to hypnosis wherein the subconscious mind responds to "outer" suggestion, i.e., "you hate cigarettes and ice cream". Hypnosis is resorted to, because one erroneously accepts for fact, his inability to consciously choose that which he now desires. We have accredited a great deal of power to those decisions which we ourselves have consciously made. When a new resolution is made, it is obvious that both potentials (possibilities) exist in the mind. Through the realization that the conscious mind is, and always has been, the absolute determiner of the final accepted outcome, the will power of the individual can come into play with a new sense of self strength. The term "will power" in itself indicates an inner battle, but the will power is the strength to choose new ways, with the realization that we consciously chose (past) that which we now hold to be true (present). It becomes a matter of consciously choosing new beliefs that conform to the way we wish to be NOW. It should not be necessary to resort to hypnosis, wherein another person suggests new concepts, to the subconscious mind. When this is done one is actually hiring someone to tell him what to believe.

To reprogram the subconscious mind regarding your sense of self worth, imagine your mind as being composed of two aspects; the conscious aware mind, and the proposed subconscious repository, that you yourself have programmed. This viewing of the subconscious mind brings control back to your NOW Center of Awareness. Realize that you have programmed unsuportive ways into the subconscious and that you have the capabilities to reprogram.

SELF PERSPECTIVE

To "know thyself" must mean to know the malignancy of one's own instincts and to know as well one's power to deflect it.

KNOW THYSELF

There can be no intelligence comparable to the intelligence of self knowledge. For all things that we do are influenced by the self image that one carries with him. Blindness to one's own psychological make-up causes him to mistake emotional illusion for reality of self. The self image that one has identified with through automatic emotional reactions is an "adopted" self image.

Approach this venture with the open trusting mind of your child self, aided with a sense of humor (ability to laugh at yourself). "Hang loose" regarding your self image. Never allow self condemnation to accompany these self insights. Simply observe the manner that you have "chosen" to feel at that moment. Self condemnation is what caused your problems in the beginning and forced you to surpress these aspects of yourself from your conscious observation.

The mental and physical strength is sapped through the energy it takes to support belief in the false self image. This conflicting self is born of illusion and lives an imaginary existance. It formed upon the natural (nature-all) self from the influences of the duality based physical world. To completely dispose of comparisons in a material world is not possible as we must retain certain structures for guidance. When this comparison infringes upon the peace of mind, when it drains the spirit and the will and takes the joy from life, it is time to release the bonds of the false self image. It is time to gather the forces of mind and draw to the true Center of self awareness.

Dr. Karl Menninger

SELF PERSPECTIVE

The following chart is composed of four oppositionaly based "Zones" directly related to major emotional divisions in self.

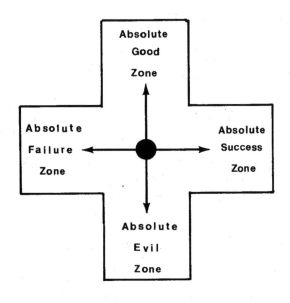

Self Identification

One does not dispassionately observe the existance of Good and Evil, Failure and Success, possibilities apart from himself. He identifies with each aspect of these four cardinal references through personal experiences that led him to harbor particular beliefs regarding himself.

PSYCOLOGICAL BEHAVIOUR MODES

The well known masks of TRAGEDY and COMEDY of the theater are easily identified with the INNER and OUTER Modes of CONFIDENCE and DOUBT. The four behaviour modes as demonstrated in Four Fold Simultaneous Contrast, elaborate on this theme to bring an added dimension of understanding to the oppositionally based psychological makeup of the emotional aspect of the human being. We are much more than OUTER CONFIDENCE versus INNER DOUBT, we are also the HIGHER mode of INNOCENCE versus the LOWER mode of GUILT.

As stated in the area of Sensitivity Variables, each person shares an emotional structure primarily composed of four sensitivity modes. Individual personalities result from an infinite blending of these four primary modes. No two personalities are alike any more than all people look alike because they share a like physical structure. Nature provides that each person be unique in appearance and personality despite our homogeneous qualities.

No attempt at psychoanalyzing the individual personality is intended by these modal "faces", other than to demonstrate that a primary oppositionally based emotional structure is shared by all. This basic conflicting division of the emotional aspects of self are of interest for the advantages that are to be gained through self understanding.

Do not identify others in these "faces" for they are a mirror image of yourself. When you observe one of these aspects being demonstrated by another, simply observe; "I do that too". This will bring the meaning of compassion to you and further insight into yourself.

It is unpleasant to be psychoanalyzed by another when one has not requested this intrusion on self. It is all too simple to believe we "know" how another person feels. The inclination to project our own interpretation onto the outer world makes this psychoanalyzing a very risky venture indeed, as we tend to see in another person what we want to see. When this is done, the other person as we see him, is a figment of our imagination and exists to us only as we have projected him to be.

Cardinal Reference Points Are "Borrowed" From:
"Material Perspective" Cardinal Reference Points

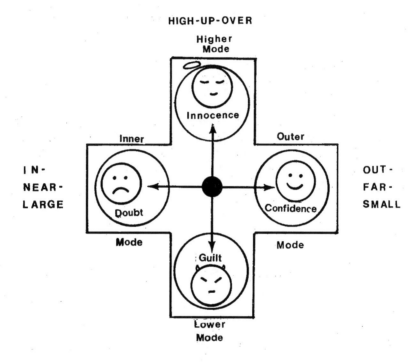

● **Center Observation Of Divided Self Aspects**

These Modes evolved from the Sensitivity Variables and carry within themselves the meaning of the facets and progress to exemplify further demonstrations of the divided conflicting emotional psyche.

Absolute "Good" Zone

IN THE HIGH-UP-ABOVE PERSPECTIVE POSITION IS THE:

HIGHER MODE OF SELF INNOCENCE
Predominate Positive Content

One mentally pictures himself containing a "higher" aspect of self that is associated with all that is seen as "good" in self. This "good" self is symbolized by a halo to represent Innocence. This mode also serves in a self elevating capacity in which one may view himself as "better than" someone else.

Absolute "Evil" Zone

IN THE LOW-DOWN-UNDER PERSPECTIVE POSITION IS THE:

LOWER MODE OF SELF GUILT
Predominate Negative Content

The lower modal aspect of self acts in direct opposition to the higher aspect of self. This lower aspect is embellished with the horns of Satan, symbolic of all self aspects viewed as evil. The lower mode of self is experienced as guilt. This mode is also a self demeaning aspect of self that may feel that he is "not as good as" someone else.

Ultimately each of these zones must be classified as Predominate Positive (containing both positive and negative aspects) and Predominate Negative (containing both negative and positive aspects) for while they represent defined divisions, each of these divisions are in themselves ambivalent* in nature. This form of ambivalance is more clearly defined in a forthcoming discussion of "Isolated Modes".

HIGHER
PREDOMINATE POSITIVE

Innocence

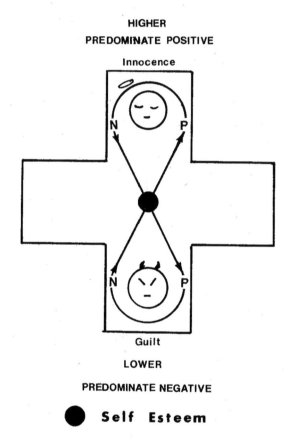

Guilt

LOWER

PREDOMINATE NEGATIVE

● **Self Esteem**

*Ambivalent, simultaneous conflicting feelings.

Absolute "Failure" Zone

OCCUPYING THE OUT-FAR-SMALL PERSPECTIVE POSITION:

OUTER MODE OF SELF CONFIDENCE
Predominate Positive Content

Because the Outer Mode, symbolized by the bright smiling face of self confidence seemingly contradicts this "Out Far Small " position, it is necessary to acknowledge the "front" that one frequently assumes in order to face outer conditions. Although this "front" represents self confidence it also contains an element of pretense that all is well with this person. One feels small and insignificant when faced with the complex matter of finding his place in society and working to maintain it. This "front" is projected as a cover up for one's inner feelings of inadequacy.

Absolute "Success" Zone

IN THE IN-NEAR-LARGE PERSPECTIVE POSITION:

INNER MODE OF SELF DOUBT
Predominent Negative Content

Each person is the "most important person" in the world to himself and as such is naturally "largely" concerned with self. In direct opposition to Out Far Small (Outer Self Confidence) is the Inner aspect of self. The Inner self is symbolized by a tearful downcast face as self doubt is encountered. (The Inner Mode of self is not to be confused with the Center of self.)

The INNER and OUTER modes reflect personal feelings of Self Confidence and Self Doubt within society's Success-Failure structure that is based on competition and evaluation. Each person estimates his own value according to his material successes and failures. Conflicts underlying the Higher and Lower modes, "surface" within the emotional experiences of the Outer Confidence and the Inner Doubt divisions. The degree of conflict experienced by the divisions of the Higher and Lower aspects become apparent in one's particular ability to achieve a balanced (centered) position in self as related to adjustment in society.

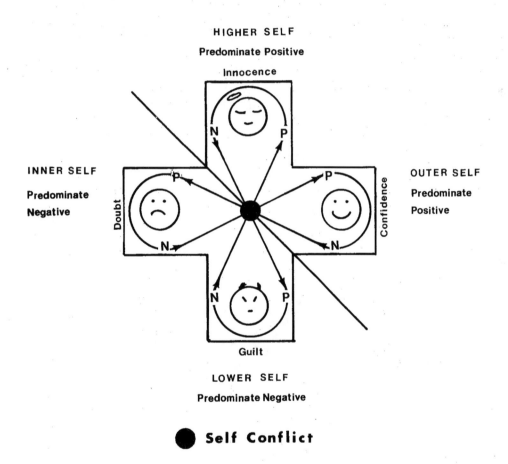

HIGHER SELF

Predominate Positive

Innocence

INNER SELF

Predominate
Negative

OUTER SELF

Predominate
Positive

Guilt

LOWER SELF

Predominate Negative

● Self Conflict

The major division of the psyche is demonstrated by these two "halves" of self engaged in private battle. The degree of "division" varys with the indvidual. Each person is the only one who can know the extent of the division existing within himself.

107

Conflict is also experienced between the Higher (innocent) and the Lower (guilty) modes in the area of emotions termed "conscience"; one's personal persuasion to do the "right" thing. One's conscience and the laws established by society do not necessarily have the same origin. Laws indicate forcing one into obeidience. Conscience refers to the "choice" in self that one believes to be the right thing to do; his personally adopted moral code of ethics.

The Outer and Inner Modes are acting participants of this conflict as one's conscience is active in all phases of life. This can be illustrated as the moral code one carries into any contest in life that determines his methods of winning. For instance, some people will cheat for the thrill of winning, while others would rather lose than subject themselves to the self punishment that arises upon feeling guilty. This guilt has nothing to do with whether one is caught cheating but is strictly a matter of self punishment for violating his own moral code.

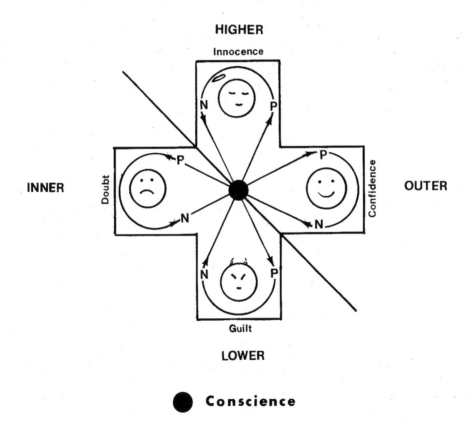

Conscience

To follow one's own moral code, strictly, would be to eradicate feelings of guilt. If a person who has decided right from wrong is satisfied that he has done the correct thing, there can be no inner conflict. An effort to "please" society somethimes results in decisions made against one's principles. One may also violate his own moral code in a fearful effort to provide a sense of material security.

Society dictates that we first, love our neighbor, and secondly, that we be kind, unselfish and pure. While one may sincerely attempt to be all of these things, these rules violate human nature and no one succeeds one hundred per cent. The next best thing then, is to hope to "appear" to be these things as requested by society.

MENTAL BLOCK

(DIVIVED SELF)

MENTAL BLOCK · DIVIDED SELF

Self disapproval is experienced as we erroneously believe we are supposed to be perfect and we know we are not. In order to be accepted by ourselves and others, we give our all to preserve a picture as close to perfection as we can. We attack this hopeless task in grim earnest. We must somehow convince ourselves and others that we are "good" and "acceptable in all ways, as we attempt to conceal any aspect that is not acceptable to the self. Even if we could live only as a perfect person, it is not likely that anyone would like us, as we would not fit in with the human race. Even though this is an impossible goal and we would not be liked if we achieved it, we refuse to give up the attempt to convince ourselves and others that we are such a person.

The initial division of the two inclusive opposites is again defined as one attempts to "block" from self view those aspects of himself that he personally finds objectionable. This blocking maneuver is shown as:

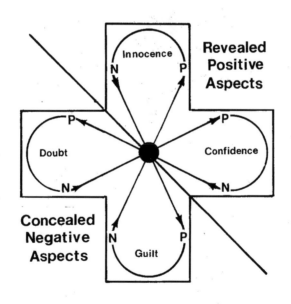

● **Self Deception**

ILLUSIONARY SELF IMAGE

All of life's emotional experience cannot be the peaceful experience such as when we view beautiful things. This type of emotional experience requires no effort on our part, as these experiences are given to us as a birthright. Life would be dull indeed without them. There are many self destructive emotions, however, that we could live happier, and longer, without. Each unpleasant emotion stems from a direct lack of true understanding of the self. We can learn to see "beauty" in all aspects of life through the realization that we do create our own emotional reality, even when that reality is not so pleasant. The manner in which we choose to see reality, is not a fixed immovable thing. Our adverse emotional experiences will change when we choose to "see" differently.

It is the writer's aim to convince the reader that he is the final determiner of his own self worth, as well as being in a central position of full control over all of his emotional experiences. A methodical form of repetition has evolved as a matter of necessity in bringing this message clearly home to the reader. If one example does not cause this awareness, possibly another one will.

ILLUSIONARY SELF IMAGE

Summary

SELF CENTERED - CENTERED SELF

Human beings are Centered in Self as a simple phenomena of nature. It is not possible to be "other centered", yet each thing that we do must appear to be selfless. This is a tremendous burden that we bear. The reprimand that we all heard as children, "Don't be selfish", led us to believe that recognizing self before others is a shameful thing. Knowledge as to one's position in regard to others must become first, knowledge of self. One must be "Centered in Self" before he truly understands the meaning of self centeredness as it truly applies to him. Accusations such as, "You only think of yourself, Why don't you think of me?" exhibits a mutual state of self centeredness. In our "guilty" condition, we do not see clearly enough to recognize the implications of such statements.

•••

Each person exists as he imagines himself to be. He lives totally in the world of his own mind while he uses the outer world as a mirror in which to view himself. He falsely assumes that others are as aware of him as he is. This is not so. Each is completely taken up with his own existance. This is not merely a self centered condition but rather a natural phenomena of the Centered Self which comes about as a matter of necessity as we are not equipped to see through the eyes of another.

As the center of his universe each must feel that he is capable of existing as a competent individual who has arrived at the correct answers to all questions. Again, this is not merely an egocentric trait but is an absolute necessity for the survival of the organism. If we did not feel that we basically had the majority of the correct answers to survive we would not survive. This set of answers constitute our personal belief structures. These structures provide orientation to all outer conditions. We have assumed a mental identification of ourselves and all other things that will guide us through our material lives. When anyone or anything, threatens our self identifications, fear of self anniliation is experienced. Again, this is not a surface egotistical thing, but a very necessary need to KNOW, to be oriented. To be disoriented means to be lost. Lost to oneself. This fear is equally as fundamental as the fear of death.

DUALITY

These combined two aspects; the need to know, and the need go be "good", result in a false self image who believes himself to have all of the correct answers, plus he believes he is all things that are good and admirable. Without exception, each person carries these beliefs about himself.

In stark contrast, each person also carries the seeds of self doubt. In his heart he does not believe the story he has told himself regarding his perfect self picture. This doubt is every bit as strong as the opposite self confidence he harbors. He is torn between these two self pictures he carries. These opposites are not vague shadowy feelings but are two strongly opposing convictions regarding self condition.

The negative views of self are surpressed, and one may or may not admit to them on a conscious level. For the most part, he does not admit to the negative aspects but wages a battle against the outer world while attempting to "prove" his self worth, in the hopes of ceasing the inner conflict. If outer conditions such as a loving mate, loving children, respective superiors, etc., all reflect him favorably he moves along, content on the surface and it is only in moments of silence that his self doubt whispers to him. He makes sure he does not experience many moments of silence and surrounds himself with people and activity to avoid such encounters with himself. The fear of being alone is based on this foundation, for if we are not distracted we may turn upon self and sense the underlying fear that lies below the surface.

One may believe he is fighting the outer world, but in truth he is engaged in private battle with himself. As he uses the outer world for self reflection, he sometimes sees the negative aspects of himself that he tries so desperately to hide from himself. When this happens, he becomes very angry at the source of self exposure.

When living from a picture of self perfection, and the need of constant reassurance from other people, as well as success in material things to reflect this self perfection, he is courting self destruction. His very life depends upon preserving this false self image because he believes he IS this false self image. This image is his very orientation and he knows no other. His picture perfect self image is as inflexible as a pane of glass and can do nothing but shatter when struck. He suffers deep humiliation when he is severely chastized and is no longer able to identify with his idolized self. This person is actually disoriented and may become violent in retaliation at the "injustice" as he sees it. This shattered, disoriented self is potentially capable of murder, which at this point is associated in his mind with self preservation, the strongest of all human instincts. He may feel justified in the act of murder, as he himself has been destroyed.

THE "BEAST" BORN OF ILLUSION

In order to rid ourselves of this "beast" that lives within us, we must first recognize that he is there, in one degree or another, in each and every one of us. The beast evolves from beliefs that we must be perfect, successful, and above all reproach. The beast is the imagined perfect self. He simply does not exist except in the imagination of each person. He is "shocked" at the outrageous conduct of others in which they appear to to be selfish, grasping, and cruel. He is self justification that blinds one to the reality that all people are basically the same, containing all those things that he himself contains. He is the barrier that keeps us from understanding and accepting ourselves and others as imperfect human beings. He is hate, he is revenge, he is judgment. He grew rigid and demanding of the material world as self evaluation unfolded and found itself lacking. His name is fear, fear for self survival. He is not survival, instead, he is self destruction pure and simple, as he pours forth bitterness, hate, and violence against himself and others.

SELF ACCEPTANCE

When one suffers public humiliation he may feel that "he" is the object of the ridicule and judgment of his peers. In truth, others are only vaguely aware of his experiences and will notice him only momentarily as he passes in their line of vision. It is true that the general public ridicules people who have ignored the laws of required perfection, however, this ridicule stems directly from their own fears and does not indicate that they are concerned with the other person as such. They quickly become preoccupied with their own centered self state and the many humiliations that one may relive in his mind, as a result of his failures, belong solely to him and do not occupy the minds of others as he may believe.

You have only to accept yourself to obtain release from the evaluations of society. You have only to accept yourself in your shared condition of the imperfect human, to experience life from the "whole" center of self. Forgiveness and acceptance of a much higher nature lives within your heart and when you release the false beliefs that you carry regarding your self identification, you will come to know it, and to live from it as a source of inner orientation, a balance not dependent on the proving of self, but of simple acceptance of self requiring no proof.

UNIT

C

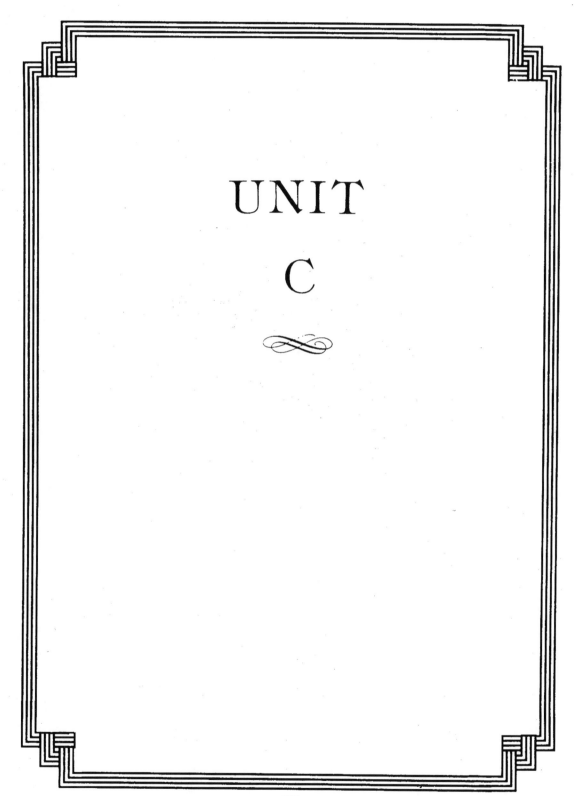

VARIABLE ADAPTIVE FRONT

Through our idealized picture of ourselves, we tend to believe that we ourselves, are peace loving individuals that ask no more of the world than to be left in our peace. But alas, "others" will not allow this. We are forced to fight for our existance, then and only then do we express anger. This is believed to be "rightful" anger. In truth this is the only anger there is, as each person feels the same, and as each person exercises his "rights", anger becomes a demonstrated aspect of human nature.

VARIABLE ADAPTIVE FRONT

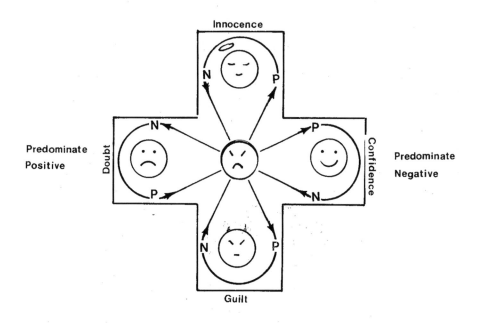

Predominate Positive

Innocence

Predominate Positive

Doubt

Confidence

Predominate Negative

Guilt

Predominate Negative

● **Focused Emotion: Anger**

The subtleties of nature have provided each person with an individual physical appearance; facial features and physical structure. Each person "adopts" his own emotional face. This face is the "front" that one presents to the exterior world and reflects his self image. The "Front" previously referred to in the area of projected self confidence, is only one of the faces that one assumes, for as one projects his particular personality, many different "fronts" are required for facing varying situations. It is through these varying situations that "Isolated Modes" become recognizable personal experience.

ISOLATED

SELF IMAGE MODULATORS

Four "modulators" serve a dual purpose within the oppositionally based emotional system. First, viewed in a technical manner they allow for emotional transition from one modal zone to another, much as a similiar concept of a modulator (as in musical composition) is used to pass from one key to another through the use of a chord common to both.

The modulators must be defined as containing both positive and negative aspects directly related to the neighboring zones. This is done to further clarify the underlying oppositionally based emotional system, however, the emotional makeup as experienced by each person is much too complex to be defined in set terms. It must be remembered that each of these modulator "faces" contain aspects of each of the other modulators, as well as each of the other modes. For instance, self pity can have an infinite number of underlying emotional facets. It is this personal emotional interpretation of all things that culminate in the unique personality of each person. For this reason, it would not be possible to stipulate in exact terms the emotional origin or content of each of the modes or the modulators as they apply to any two people, let alone all people.

Obvious emotional confusion, however, is exemplified by these "isolated" faces. For instance, self pity; regardless of the personal reasons for this experience is a "strength robbing" emotion to any one who experiences it as a "focused" emotion.

Secondly, the modulators serve as "adaptors" as one uses these four "self image preservors" as a protection against the outside world. As previously stated, each person must basically feel that he is good and acceptable in all ways. These modulators serve to provide this basic self acceptance on a superficial level. While this form of emotional protecttion provides for a certain degree of adjustment, it does not provide peace of mind from conflicts resulting from these self bolstering methods.

ISOLATED MODULATORS

A SMILE HAS MANY MEANINGS,
AS ALSO DOES A TEAR,
THE HALO MAY BE MASQUERADE,
TO ALLIVIATE A FEAR.

Experiencing traumatic emotional reactions signified by any of these "Isolated" modulators indicates that one is living from a false self image. A decision to eradicate these emotional "games" that one plays against himself will eventually result in a mind free of the emotional turmoil these aspects perpetuate.

As can be observed in the above descriptions of the modulators: each modulator conveys two slightly different connotations. The reason for these differences are shown on the two following charts.

Innocence

SELF
ENOBLEMENT

N

P

SELF PITY

VULNERABLE
ANGER

SELFISHNESS
LOOKING OUT

N

P

FOR #1

Guilt

⬤ Innocence Vs. Guilt

The Isolated Modulators of the Innocence-Guilt Cycle exhibit facets of
the human emotional personality that one prefers not to recognize in
self. With the possible exception of "vulnerable anger" one is more inclined to see these aspects demonstrated by others, and may "project"
these aspects on others even when this may not be the case. We must
*"Cast the gleam out of our own eyes" in order that we can clearly see
another.

These same Isolated Modulators assume slightly different connotations descriptive of an emotional nature containing admirable aspects and several perhaps not so admirable, but more acceptable to self. These variances are mentally superimposed over the less to be desired aspects for self viewing.

POTENTIAL ASPECTS OF:

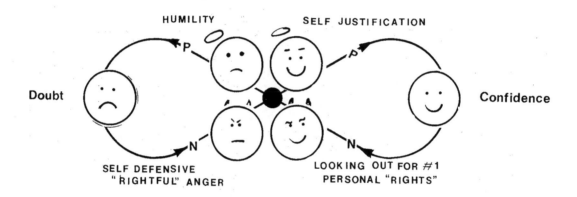

Self Doubt Vs. Self Confidence

These eight isolated modulators are not demonstrations of the baser aspects of humanity; they are the emotional disturbances that evolve from one's own conviction that he has a baser aspect.

Since there are no universal absolute determiners defining "good" as opposed to "bad", this baser aspect of the self can only be a resolution of each individual in respect to himself.

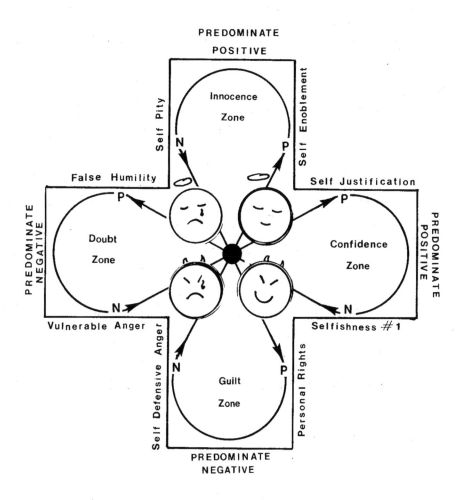

On the above chart the Isolated Modes meld together. The combined forms are actuated through the particular placement of the modulators in relation to neighboring zones.

ISOLATED MODULATOR DEFINITIONS

These Isolated Modulators are used as spring boards of thought pointing out the most obvious self misconceptions. As with the origin of these facets themselves, it is not possible to completely separate one from another in the discussion of each. One can observe underlying "neighboring" facets surfacing when one attempts to do this, however, recognition of personal identification with any specific mode or modulator, while experiencing emotional discomfort, indicates that one is not "centered" in his emotions and is supporting the false self image to an emotionally disabling degree. The false self image cannot live within the light and as you continue to focus light upon him he will disappear into nothingness. Do not feel guilt as you recognize his tactics, as he thrives on guilt, it is an active part of his nature.

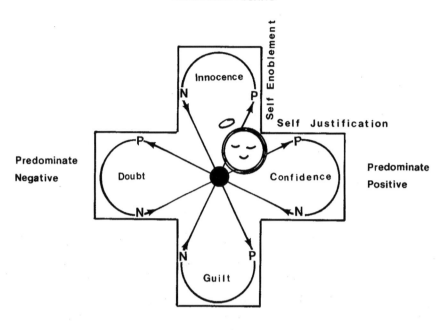

Predominate Positive

Self Enoblement

Innocence

N   P

Self Justification

P   P

Doubt   Confidence

N   N

Predominate Negative   Predominate Positive

N   P

Guilt

Predominate Negative

● **Self Enoblement**
Self Justification

The particular placement of this isolated modulator on the above chart is evidential of it's psuedo Double Positive content. This Double Positive influence bolsters one's self confidence as based on a "blind" viewing of one's self. While this viewing of self is a "pleasant" experience, minus "conscious" conflict, it prompts one to indulge in futile arguments in behalf of his beliefs in an effort to convince himself and others that he is "right" at all times.

GUILT

Terms defined as: "Society's Evil" in respect to self, may go unrecognized because almost no one will admit to having this aspect potential. When we do a "wrong" thing as interpreted by self judgment, we must rationalize and rearrange the happening in our mind until we can comfortably put this wrong doing in a higher aspect of self: "Circumstances were out of my control......", "I did it in the name of justice......", "I balanced the scales in my own way......", etc. The only valid evil is believed by the self, to be committed by someone else. The word "Evil" is used for describing the actions of others.

Personal suffering (guilt) takes place until one has convinced himself that any wrong doing by the self is justified and therefore becomes excusable if not actually noble. It states in the bible that: "One goes to Hell when he dies if he has been evil". Whether we believe in hell or not, we fear punishment of some kind. "I therefore must convince myself that what I do is justified and I find myself "Not Guilty". This is obviously only fooling the self. There can be but one hell, and that is one of a confused mind doling out self punishment. Each "creates" his own hell in this manner, for we have the power to light the fires of hell in our own souls.

It is vitally important for mental health to realize that each person, as an expression of life, contains the POTENTIAL of doing and expressing any aspect of life, if the conditions around him apply sufficient pressure. This is a very difficult point to grasp and apply to the self, but if it can be done, will literally free a mind of guilt feelings. This does not mean that you will express all aspects of life, for you will not. If you are fortunate enough to be spared the agony of having committed any of the so called sins of the human race, but observe another's guilt, remember: "But for the grace of God, there go I." Say a prayer of peace for the offender and give thanks that you have not been tried to do this thing.

Judging of the evil of others is a direct indication of self conflict and is done only as a means of bolstering one's own shaky feelings of self confidence or self worth. Insisting that others behave according to your moral code is a method of assuring yourself that you do have valid opinions. If one accepts himself fully as he is now, he can then accept others as they are now. When you can look at another, observe what he is doing and it carries no personal meaning to you, when his actions do not bring an emotionally adverse reaction from you, then and only then, are you living from your true center. Any time lost in judging others is time lost in which you could be freeing yourself from your own mental bondage.

> Every day, is Judgment Day,
> As we stand in public judgment of others,
> And secret judgment of ourselves.

All judgments of others pay off in self bolstering beliefs such as: "I could never do the evil he did, therefore I am a better person than he." This indicates a need to bolster one's own self worth at the expense of another. Or taking it upon one's self to call the actions of another evil in the name of God. It can only be your evaluation of what is evil and to assume that there is one good; your good, in the name of God, is self defeating.

Observe that you have a personal belief structure of what is "right" and what is "wrong". Observe that you have a good many qualities that belong in both categories according to your very own judgment. You have these qualities because you are human. Remember that all things will be evident among the masses as a whole, from the sublime to the profane, these potentials reside in each human being. Attempt to consciously recognize the thoughts and deeds of your own that you would have to place in the lower aspect of yourself and then forgive yourself for being human. When this aspect of your self is fully recognized and accepted as a part of your human condition, there will be no self judgment. A sincere acceptance of yourself in your imperfect human condition will free you from a heavy feeling of guilt that you may have carried with you for a lifetime. At the same instant you cease judgment upon yourself, you will cease judgment upon others.

An interesting fact is that much of what the average person does that could be considered evil, is done as a result of attempting to appear good. Acts that are committed to avoid exposure are often worse than the original "sin". It is not a sin to be human. We are not sinners bowing before a perfect judging God. We carry the spirit of God within us and the only sin is to be ignorant of our true natures.

You may be thinking, "But what of all the 'real' evil out there? Don't we have to do something about that?" There isn't any real evil out there. "There is nothing either good or bad but thinking makes it so".* We can aid another in their time of need, but we cannot discern evil, for it wears no recognizable face to all.

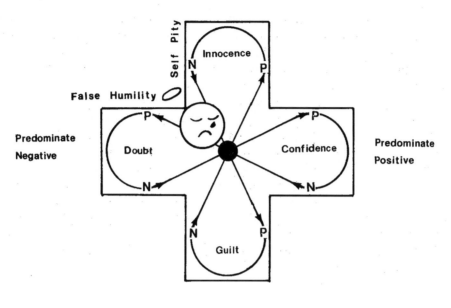

Predominate Positive

Self Pity

Innocence

False Humility

Doubt

Confidence

Predominate Negative

Predominate Positive

Guilt

Predominate Negative

Self Pity
False Humility

Self Pity, as placed on the chart, exhibits direct Positive-Negative content which acts as a psuedo balancing agent. When one indulges in self pity, he is viewing himself as innocent and deserving, but has been denied his just dues. Sometimes a trend toward self doubt arises from this outer denial. When this is the case, self pity is counter balanced with feelings of superiority toward those who do not recognize his "goodness".

The inferior doubtful self may also receive his condolences from being "humble". He feels that to be meek guarantees him a reward in heaven. This very meekness takes on a feeling of superiority as one, while seeing himself as meek, is relegating himself to the kingdom of heaven, which therefore makes him feel superior to others in his own eyes. He becomes caught in the trap of the opposites through no fault of his own other than he does not comprehend his true position of equality with all others. In this way feelings of superiority become a part of the negative doubtful self also.

LONELY ?

When one experiences life limited by comparison thinking only, other people exist solely as determiners of his own personal status. In this manner we do not see the other person as he is, but only as he compares to us; how he makes us feel about ourselves. The resulting self judgment or self enoblement causes us to act in self defeating ways. In order to bring these positive-negative aspects of self to one centered self acceptance, "comparisons" must be evaluated as being necessary structures for guidance, but not applied in the material sense to our own self worth or the worth of others. In times of emergency all people are bound together in a sense of common brotherhood regardless of material circumstances. When the emergency is over, these people revert to form and allow the shallow existance dictated by social standing to become their ruling God; the force that says this person is better than another person. We are all bound together in the common bonds of the trials and tribulations of every day life, from which no one is exempt, we need not wait until death is eminent to call each other truly our brother.

AT THE "MERCY" OF SOCIETY

One can "go to pieces" in the face of adverse exterior conditions and be "rightfully" full of self pity, or he can become "centered" in his own self strength. This will replace the weakness that comes from depending on exterior circumstances to provide support.

SELF SACRIFICE

Self pity is a form of self enoblement. One may feel that he alone carries the burdens while others go off scott free. The truth is one assumes the burdens that he "chooses" to assume for specific reasons that may not be immediately apparent on the surface.

Self sacrifice may seem a noble (positive) thing to do; a sacrificing of the self in favor of the comfort and well being of others. This is probably the most misunderstood of the self concieved higher aspects, for self sacrifice means self denial. One is actually giving away something that rightfully belongs to him. This type of self sacrifice may serve to cause ultimate resentment of others even though they have not arranged this situation. When one does for others while resenting it, the act does not retain its positive influence but becomes a negative trait. This negative trait is not viewed as such by the person who perpetuates this form of self sacrifice. He simply desires that others appreciate what he is giving up for them. It is not likely that others even recognize these actions as sacrifice and regard this treatment as their just due. When one encourages this form of treatment of himself he is not in a true position to object or complain regarding whatever treatment he receives from others, as he has "chosen" to act in this self abasing manner. Feelings of basic unworthiness cause one to place no regard toward himself. Servitude to others, at the expense of self, is substituted in hopes of elevating self esteem.

Do for others when you truly desire to give of yourself with no expectation of repayment. This is free giving, while retaining one's self respect.

"Do not ask of me that which I do not wish to give, for this type of giving is fearful giving; giving in hopes of return of approval from you."

Freeing another to be himself, includes a withdrawal of fearful giving. You may appear to be callous to another. How much better to appear callous than to give while resenting it. This resentment can only result in a feeling of self dislike as well as dislike for the other person.

JEALOUSY

One person is never more deserving of good fortune than another. Jealousy of another's good fortune is a self destructive emotion and can do no more than to destroy the happiness of the person who harbors it. One can always find someone who is better off or worse off than he is. In the constantly comparing manner of the human, one is always doing this. Seeing someone who has more problems than he has may enable one to face his problems better, but even this is not the final answer, as discontentment again arises upon sighting someone else's wealth. Realizing that one's total reality exists within his chosen perception frees him to experience that which he wishes, regardless of the conditions of others. An inner satisfaction comes when one fully accepts that which his life is at this moment.

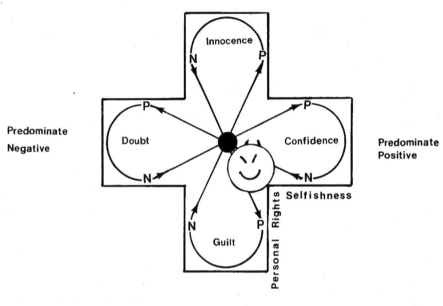

Predominate Positive

Predominate Negative

Predominate Positive

Predominate Negative

Innocence

Doubt

Confidence

Guilt

Selfishness

Personal Rights

● **Selfishness**
  Personal Rights

This modulator, as placed on the chart, exhibits direct Negative-Positive content.

Self confidence and its related "success factor", contains a guilt potential in that one must take care that he does not "get more" than another person. This type of fear is often counter-balanced by self inflicted guilt feelings wherein one "pays" for being selfish.

We have been taught to place the other person before self, however, placing one's needs and wishes before others is not always a negative thing to do as was noted in "Self Pity - Self Enoblement." It is necessary to recognize and reserve one's rights minus guilt feelings. This modulator has its negative aspects in that one may ignore the rights of others in his search for material reassurance. Certain comforts are necessary for survival and there is nothing wrong in having these things. It is when the need to amass material things to provide a form of emotional security, in the belief that the amount one "owns" provides proof of the amount of one's worth, that one may resort to unscrupulous methods of stepping on the backs of others in his climb to the top. It is obvious that some people will not feel extreme guilt at this proposal while others will. It is in this light that one may fear others will view him if he insists on his personal "rights". The difference deserves distinguishing between.

SELF CONFIDENCE

Self confidence is predominately positive, as self confidence is a very necessary ingredient to successful living, however, much of what passes for self confidence is in truth a cover up for feelings of inferiority. Confidence based on a secure feeling of self worth has nothing in common with the arrogant braggart who feels it necessary to demean others in order to feel good about himself. A bragging, bullying, egotistical, self puffed up individual is all "front". There can be nothing but a fearful self behind this mask. A true acceptance of self brings with it a true acceptance of all other people, in whatever state they have chosen. Feelings of superiority have nothing in common with true self acceptance, although they give off positive tones to the person who feels himself to be superior. Take time to notice the manner in which you determine your own self worth. See that all people are equal and that money, intelligence, etc., does not make for a "better" person. Each makes for a "different" person. You will be doing yourself, not others, a favor when you do this, as you are bound to be out done yourself in the comparison game sooner or later, as someone who appears to be "better" than you comes along to alter your self image for the worse.

To be a certain thing and not know it,
Is to vainly defend the existance,
Of a perfect illusionary self.

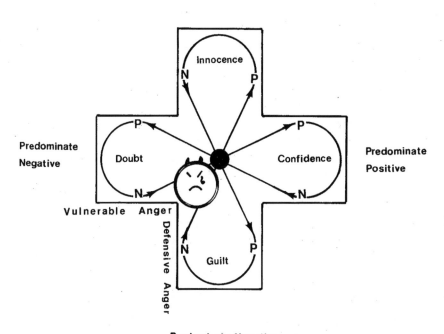

This type of anger is of double negative direct content. This is a difficult emotional state to pull one's self out of, as no direct counter balance exists in this modulator. This is the most self destructive emotion that one can "entertain". Physical attack upon another may appear to be the only solution, if the injury has been of sufficient damage to the ego.

As was previously stated, the Emotional System exhibits a constant underlying structure based on a positive-negative interaction, but the emotions experienced at any given time are the emotions that one generates for himself. While Vulnerable Anger is a mode changer, it is impossible to predict which mode one may experience upon this emotional upset. One may choose to shift to another modulator and indulge in self pity, in which case he heaps misery upon his own head as he harbors grudges and bitterness. The other person is not the recipient of the ill feeling, it is the personal experience of the self. One may feel he has a "right" to hate another but is in reality inflicting added injury upon himself. He may be incited to take defensive action which could ultimately result in experiences of the lower mode of guilt. The one thing this Isolated Modulator cannot do is provide a peaceful state of mind.

Defensive anger is projected in hopes of protecting one's "honor" (saving face.) If one insists upon retaining this false self image he can be assured of an emotionally miserable existance. Much of the anger we experience toward others is a result of an injury to the false self image. There will always be someone who will "put us down." Becoming angry at another person for this reason is an automatic response that can be eliminated by simply realizing that another person has no more power to hurt you, than you give to him.

AS ABOVE - SO BELOW

This section has been devoted to clarifications of the "hidden" self of the subconscious and the split in the psyche that results from this hidden self.

Each person lives in a state of self contradiction as a result of this division as he allows exterior conditions to determine his self position. Automatic responses result in a lack of true self determined identity wherein one remains centered in self conviction impervious to the pressures of outer dictates.

The manner in which each person experiences life, is dependent upon his personal "choices" of all existing emotional responses known to humanity. One can choose to react to outer conditions in any way that will please himself the most. It is true that some people only seem to be happy when they are sad, however, if you are experiencing personal unhappiness, you are not ultimately choosing in your own best interests.

INTEGRATION

Each consciously recognized attempt to glorify negative self aspects is a step toward total integration. Emotions in the form of anger, self pity etc., are an indication of imbalance which results from friction between your dual self pictures. Take care that you do not go to the opposite extreme of self justification and "put yourself down", as this mental action will not bring about a center balance, it only serves as an extreme emotional counter balance. In this "integration" project you may observe your emotional experiences and use this information in your behalf whereas before the experience left you nothing but confusion and unhappiness. When involved in any activity which brings about adverse extreme emotion, recognize that you are allowing yourself to be led by exterior conditions. Take conscious observation of your automatic responses and "bring yourself together" by mentally claiming your centered condition. Simply state to yourself: "I choose the Center". Keep in mind that you were "choosing" an extreme emotional experience. Eventually, with persistance, a personality change comes about as a result of this self observation. The number of emotional disturbances will decrease and you will notice that emotional extremes become fewer and farther between.

Many people choose emotional extreme because these extremes allow for feelings of self importance, they feel "alive" when experiencing extreme emotion. This agitated experience makes them feel "alive" only because they have not experienced the "aliveness" of the integrated center and so have no comparison factor. In place of this agitated emotional experience comes a feeling of warmth and security from within the self. An absolute enjoyment in observing life flowing around one becomes his emotional experience. This integrated feeling defies verbal description and any attempts to do so become awkward and inadequate. Attempts to describe this "Center sensation" to others can be confused with, and interpreted by others, as a self elevating method denoting superiority. Only the person who experiences these things knows the origin of his experience but when one makes conscious contact with the Center he is not concerned with "impressing" anyone one way or another.

There is no limit to the extent of "Center" awareness that one may ultimately expect to experience, as there exists no time in which we ourselves will attain perfection, we can only gain greater awareness of its existance.

Each person gets along with others to the exact same extent that he gets along with himself. If he is friendly, easy going and peaceful, it is because he is relaxed within himself and accepts others as he accepts himself. To love oneself really means to accept oneself. This is not an egotistical matter at all, as interpreted by some cynics of the new trend toward self understanding, because this self acceptance is not based on self perfection but rather total self acceptance of one's self as a normal imperfect human being.

SECTION THREE

As Within

So Without

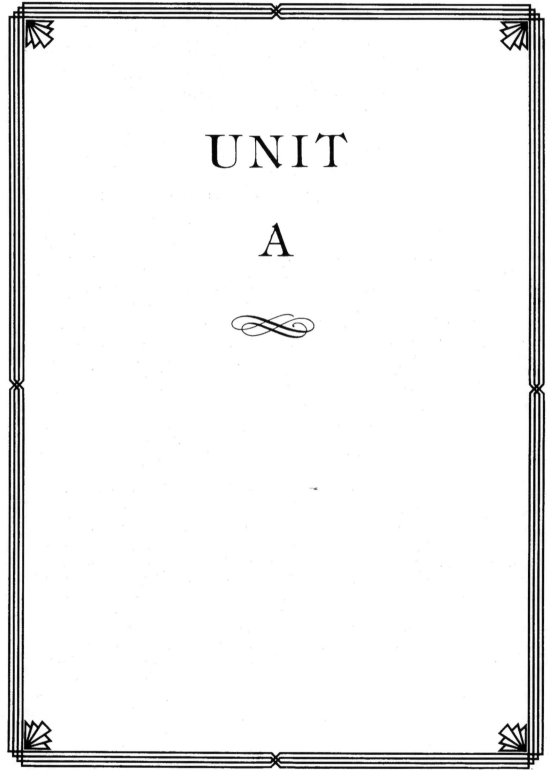

UNIT

A

Existing within each soul,
Is the never ceasing desire,
To make two things "one".
To cause a mating of the poles,
In perfect reconciliation.

THE PITFALLS OF POSITIVE THINKING

Positive thinking implies actively thinking only good thoughts which will in turn bring about only good things to the person doing the thinking. The truth is, it is not possible to think only good thoughts.

Each positive thought demands its counter negative thought. Each negative thought demands its counter positive thought. This process is endless, as one must acknowledge the two necessary points of reference before he can possibly "choose" one. To attempt to think "positive" as opposed to "negative" does not provide for a center point of choice between the two existing poles of reference.

CONTRADICTION

THE YES AND NO OF THE HUMAN MIND

In our attempts to arrive at the "proper" choice, we often arrive at no choice at all. Our lives may seem pointless because we have not "centered" in choice. It is not that we do not have the capacity of will to follow through on our choices, but that we do not clearly define our choice and follow through with it. The reason we do this is because we feel that we must cover all angles and leave nothing to chance. It is ironic that through this misconception we leave almost everything to chance. We fail to arrive at, and maintain, a central point of action wherein we do not falter. Developing a sense of trust that all is occurring for the best is mandatory in order to take the pressure off our decisions. We do not hang onto life with bleeding finger tips, we only imagine this to be so.

150

PROJECTIONS

PROJECTIONS

As beauty is in the eye of the beholder, that which is seen as ugly is also in the eye of the beholder. What one chooses to call ugly or beautiful reflects an inner condition of beauty and ugliness that is born of self enchantment or self disenchantment.

All things that you observe will not please you. There is a place for all things however. To understand how you create your reality you must see that what you observe with intense emotional dislike is an outer reflection of an inner disturbance. There is a difference in the observation of unpleasant things with a simple acceptance that such things will be, as opposed to an insistance that these things are evil or ugly. They are not evil or ugly, they just are.

All things exist, your personal experience of all things is controlled by you. The existance of heaven or hell, God or Satan, gain their form in your thoughts, as you perceive these things to be. Supernatural experiences that seemingly originate outside of the mind are actually products of the mind, by way of conscious agreement to experience these things. What the mind selects, the senses perceive. Is there, in fact, a spirit world? If you believe there is, it is so.

Experiences of Extra Sensory Perception have been agreed to by the receiver, on the consciously controlled level of thought. This conscious agreement opens channels through which insight is received. ESP is not "at the disposal" of the conscious mind at idle request, but if one keeps an open mind on this subject, he will experience a great deal more ESP experience than one who closes his mind to this aspect of thought. An open mind primes and brings forth knowledge on any subject one sincerely wishes to pursue.

"Things" are. When one views external things, minus emotional response, he is simply observing, in the impersonal manner that a camera would do. When one experiences emotional reaction toward exterior conditions, he has become a projector as well as a receiver:

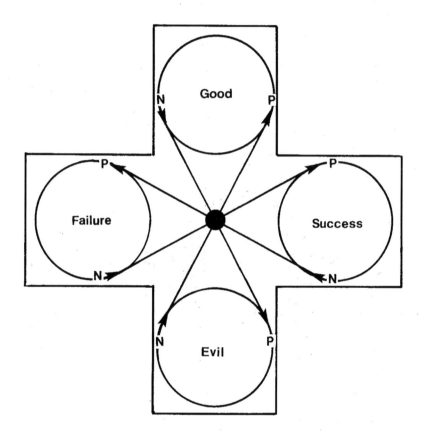

⬤ **As I Perceive It To Be- So It Is**

One "projects" his reality in the form of emotional interpretations. As emotion is a personal experience, the reality that each person perceives of is his alone.

CAUSE AND EFFECT

CAUSE AND EFFECT

That which you believe does manifest. This is not mind power separate from physical action, but the unrefutable law of Cause and Effect:

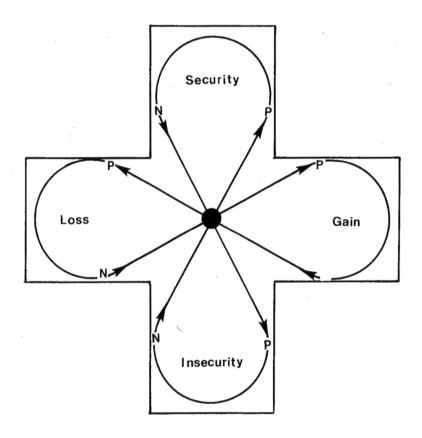

● I Am The Cause - Reality Is The Effect

CAUSE AND EFFECT

When one imagines the mind influencing things, he pictures "mind power" that will bring all that he desires to him, as if his self identity was separate from his mind action. The state of one's mind influences his experiences, in that outer conditions in his life reflect the inner condition of his mind.

The first thing that one must do to take directed control of his life, is to accept responsibility for himself. Accept the fact that the world owes you nothing. Other people are not there to provide support for you. This dependency upon other people for support is self crippling. There is no aspect of life that you cannot surmount through your own strength. Nature does not ask more of you than you are able to give.

OUR EXPERIENCES IN LIFE CONSIST OF THINGS WE HAVE AGREED TO.

This does not appear to be so because so much of what we experience we find unpleasant and unrewarding and it is difficult to believe that we have agreed to such experiences.

To have "agreed" to these conditions does not mean that we have consciously CHOSEN them, and that is the difference. When one consciously chooses his experience and follows through with the necessary supporting action, there can be no error for one is "centered" in his actions and no longer vacillates.

MOTIVATION

Through studies in the field of psychology it has been determined that mice and poeple alike respond to adequate motivation. That is, the desire to gain a particular thing causes one to become motivated to the point of action that will culminate in the achievement of the desired thing. One becomes "motivated" to action through his inability to tolerate the existing condition, whether it be a form of hunger or a form of pain.

PERSONAL TOLERANCE LEVELS

Each condition around you reflects your inner agreement. There is not one condition existing in your life that you simply will not tolerate. You actually have every aspect of your life in control. The control you have "chosen". What appears to be uncontrolled in your life is that which you have personally allowed as it did not infringe on your accepted tolerance levels to an "action motivating" degree. Each person's life styles reflect differently chosen personal tolerance levels. Everyone does not exist in like material circumstances. These differences are not a matter of "fate", but a matter of mind. When one's tolerance level, in any area of life, has been violated, his centered decision is always accompanied by "action", physical movement, to change that which he cannot tolerate.

Personal attitudes toward all aspects of life are firmly seated in the subconscious mind. Each thing that one does in his own particular way reflects his "chosen" way. Yet he is constantly in the throes of self dissatisfaction, berating himself for not accomplishing more and better things. One uses more energy feeling inadequate than he would if he had physically accomplished the desired goal. This disconnected feeling of not being in complete control of one's self comes from comparing what we have done, to what we believe we should have, or could have done. Our forces are weakened through this self disagreement.

If you are dissatisfied with the existing conditions in particular areas of your life, you may be experiencing self recrimination as you idly set higher tolerance levels than you intend to live up to. This type of thinking will not raise your tolerance levels, but is a form of wishful thinking that becomes self punishment. The areas you view as satisfactory reflect a "centered" condition in your life, a coming together of self expectation and self accomplishment. Unfortunatley, this centered self agreement is usually confined to areas that one performs in what he considers to be a superior manner.

Tolerance levels need not necessarily be changed, they need to be recognized as a reflection of one's choices, in order to bring his self expectation and his self accomplishments to a centered agreement.

RECOGNIZE EACH ACTION AS YOUR CHOICE

Accept your present tolerance levels by ceasing to compare what you have chosen to what you have not chosen. In other words, accept your own judgments to be valid. If you choose to leave a chore and go out for a day of recreation, do it without guilt feelings that come from comparing what you are doing to what you believe you should be doing. Since you have chosen otherwise what good is it to spoil your day with guilt feelings. If your personal choice does not allow for leaving the chore for leisure activity, then there is no point in berating yourself because you are unable to ignore your work. You are doing what you have chosen to do. When we recognize the fact that each thing we do is a "choice" we have made, we can experience this "chosen" activity with a "together" feeling.

If some areas of your life reflect tolerance levels that bring about major problems, you must accept the fact that you have established all conditions that remain in your life. Any conditions beyond these set rules, you simply will not tolerate. For instance if living beyond your means does not effect you adversely to an extreme degree, you will continue to live above your income.

Each person sets his own personal tolerance level for self punishment in any circumstances. We have no valid complaints regarding ill treatment from others, for as long as we are willing to tolerate these things for one reason or another, they will continue. Physical or verbal attack upon another may be the reaction when one's tolerance level has been touched upon. This is misplaced blame. We have been "asking" others to treat us as they do. Looking to the self for the reasons for tolerating ill treatment is the action that should be taken.

As one has personally created his own life style, he is obviously in the position to change that which he does not wish to remain. Determination is the key word. Some people seem to be determined to destroy themselves, others seem to be determined to surmount all obstacles. There is no "one" and no "thing" outside of the self that causes these different attitudes toward life for each person has his share of both good and bad "fortune". One can change his point of motivation through the process of taking inventory of his present habits, etc., accepting that which he chooses to remain (no one is perfect, or has to be) and applying a sincere effort to change the areas that he has allowed to exist through lack of directed action.

Recognize the fact that you are fully capable of making a decision. Refuse to mentally go over and over various possibilites. The desire to out guess the future leads to this feeling of inadequacy. Fear that one will make the wrong choice in major issues prompts inability to make a choice. There isn't any wrong or right decision, there is only the one that you make. It is not possible to see into the future and it is not possible to return to the past. One's life consists of "present moments" not yesterdays and tomorrows.

When you choose that which you wish to experience in the way of self betterment, (do not choose to make someone else over or to do your bidding, it will not work because you do not have their consent), stick to your choice in the face of all obstacles. Opposition should in no way influence one to give up on one's dreams, as is the way of many people. Exterior conditions have nothing to do with one's self determination. Ignore opposition from exterior conditions and continue with the centered desire. That which you wish to experience, you shall ultimately experience through the laws of cause and effect. When outer obstacles are met with, it is pointless to scatter one's forces by losing control through anger at the world; so called harsh reality. Observe the condition and decide which is the shortest route, over it or around it. These should be your only choices. To cease action and beat one's head against the obstacle can only result in a battered head. If you feel that you exist in a battered condition much of the time you would do well to "determine" to integrate your self strength. See your success as conditional to your self strength, not outer conditions. This will remove your tenseness regarding the outcome of any particular happening. You "know" you will overcome, and are not dependent on any particular circumstance for your security as you carry your security within yourself.

WINNER - LOSER

There exists no such person that can be defined as a "winner" as opposed to "loser", for today's winner can be tomorrow's loser. No person is without their winning qualities and their losing qualities. It is unreal to expect that one will "win" all of the time. It is just as unreal to believe that one will "lose" all of the time. Each person's life is composed of experiences characteristic of both of these conditions.

These "winning"- "losing", aspects are potentials of each person, as well as potentials of circumstances that surround this person. His personal adaptability determines his emotional reality in these areas. The correct attitude can cause one to "feel like a winner" all of the time, for he does not emotionally compete against himself, or the outer world. In other words, his happiness does not rest solely in his "winning" abilities. Ironically, this winning "feeling" in turn brings with it more material successes.

Most of the "hard facts" of life are not outside ourselves but are contained in our refusal to accept ourselves as anything less than perfect and the following conclusion that all should be perfect outside of ourselves also. Life is not rigid and hard. Our mind's are.

RICH MAN - POOR MAN

Poverty is a state of mind. When one is starving a piece of bread represents wealth. When one owns empires he feels he needs one more empire in order to feel materially secure. What represents wealth is that which we haven't got, therefore, poverty is a state of mind from which there can be no material fulfillment.

The myth of the "good" poor person is just a myth. When the poor man receives bread, he wants meat, when he receives meat he wants a cattle ranch, when he acquires the ranch he wants to own the state, then the country, then the world. The poor man and the rich man are psycholoically the same man in different material circumstances.

ALL MEN ARE CREATED EQUAL - IT IS THE MIND OF MAN THAT CREATES IMBALANCE.

Failure is a state of mind. Reality says that the rich man owns the poor man body and soul. Only if the poor man believes this to be true is it so. No manner of work is demeaning to the human. The mental state that accompanies the work (or any material situation) may cast inferior reflections onto these occupations. The physical activity is not demeaning, the mental activity is. What each person finds himself doing can be viewed by himself to be what it is, a job to be done that he is doing. No one can ask more of himself than this. In this way he has succeeded. One has to answer only to himself.

FLOW - DON'T FIGHT

Many of the problems that each person experiences are a direct result of his own interpretations of the structures of society and not the frame itself. The structures of society exert an influence on the development of the individual, however, the individual's ability to think for himself is also a determining factor. So that while "structures" of civilization exist, they do not determine the emotional experience within these structures.

These are self willed. One need not be emotionally intimidated by the money oriented mass "mind" of the people. This power syndicate is composed of individual people, all out to "buy" happiness.

Fighting the "establishment", so to speak, is a waste of your energy and can only result in a battle that you yourself perpetuate. Peace of mind will never come while one fights with anthing or anybody.

Someone once said, "I'll have peace if I have to fight for it". This has its humorous aspects but is also a vicious circle that one gets into, and for the most part doesn't realize that he is indeed going around in an endless circle. If each person can find peace within himself there would be no wars. You can pray for salvation of humanity as a whole, but you can "work" toward your own salvation. In this way you will adding to and thereby drawing closer, the existance of a peaceful world.

This may seem to be a "pollyanna" approach to solving one's problems but when one realizes that there are no other solutions and he is exhausted from searching in baron territory he will welcome this open door that leads to his freedom.

QUINTESSENCE

The "Real" You

We have all seen movies and stage plays wherein an actor gives a performance that is so convincing that we cannot believe that this person exists separate from this role. This type of performance is not really "acting" as the performer has drawn on his potential to be all things, and has "brought life" to the role in the form of "becoming" this person.

This is a very provocative thought that can be applied to the self, for each person has "chosen" the role that he plays in the world of reality. If you are completely satisfied being the person that you have chosen to be, then you have chosen wisely. If you are not, there is nothing to stop you from claiming new ways to be and "becoming" these things that you wish to "bring to life". The potential to be any expression of life that you can "imagine" yourself being, lives within you. Put this aspect of yourself into overt (open-public) action. You are not pretending, this really is an aspect of yourself that you have not developed because you thought you could not.

QUINTESSENCE

THE QUINTESSENCE OF EACH PERSON IS THAT SAME PERSON
MINUS HIS SELF DISSATISFACTIONS.

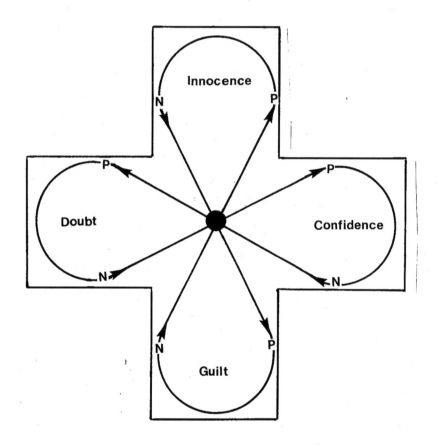

● **Quintessence**

The quintessence of each person is: "The most perfect manifestation or embodiement of that person"; the best that you are of all of the things that you are. Each person has something of unique value to offer the world that no one else could possibly do. One must be aware of his potential to the fullest degree. The only limitations that we have are the ones we set for ourselves.

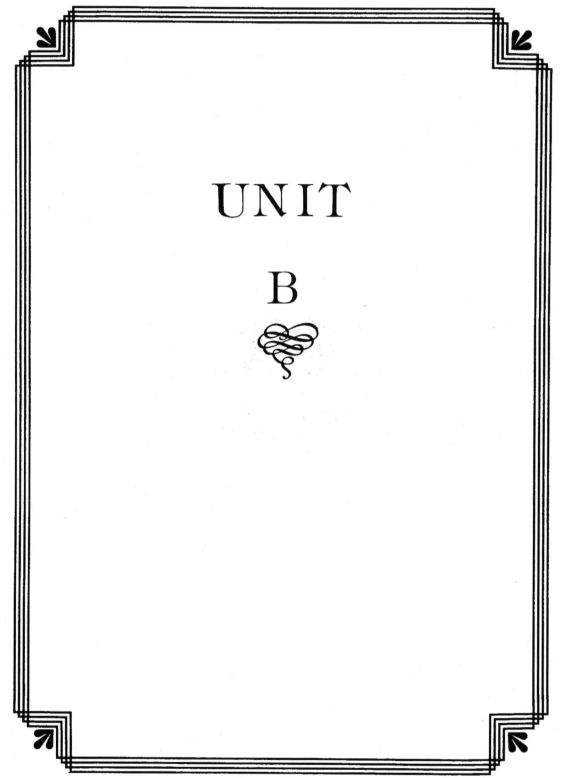

UNIT

B

SOLITARY PROJECTIONS

IMAGINATION

WORRY

Unleashed imagination plays a large part in the worry cycle. When one worrys he actually projects frightening mental images to the foreground of his mind and then observes these dire possibilities as real tangible happenings. The resulting emotional experience is the same as if they were actually happening as this "focus" of consciousness becomes one's present reality. Whether or not this thing ever takes material form, it has been an actual mental-physical experience of the person who is subjecting himself to these self destructive emotions. Each thing that we have ever imagined has been a part of our reality, for the only reality that we can ever know is the experience of our own mind.

DAYDREAMS

Daydreams are the opposite mental occupation of worry. Here we deliberately create favorable exciting situations to "experience". Unleashed imagination is employed here as we view to our hearts content all that we desire to be. When not carried to excess, in that all one does is daydream, these mental meanderings have a favorable balancing effect on the system.

CHOICE

Observation of the existance of these solitary projections ,worry and daydreaming, indicate the ability of the mind to choose that which it will experience. Each has been choosing his own happiness or unhappiness all of his life.

Mental control should be seen at this point for what it is, common sense, as it is senseless to destroy one's own peace of mind. One can become alerted to the fact that he is using his mental powers against himself by deciding to monitor his emotional experiences. Request this alerting action of your subconscious mind and you will not be allowed to remain "asleep" while automatic responses take their toll on you. Nine tenths of the battle is won upon recognizing the fact that you are perpetuating your discomfort by providing the necessary attention to continue its existance.

It is possible to disolve a particular mood that one is not enjoying, such as anxiety, depression, or simply the blahs. First realize that the exterior world is not "out of balance", others do not feel as you do. This emotional disturbance is yours alone. Through your own interpretive mind you have "created" this upset within yourself. STOP! Look at the mood you have "created" In order to do this, you must stop "giving it life" long enough to see it for what it is, a personal creation of your own mind that has no reality other than you have given it. While you are observing the mood as separate from yourself, the automatice response system is short circuited. This type of emotion is self hyptnotism, the replaying of circumstances in the mind until one no longer looks away from the depressing mental picture but becomes this imagined situation to the extinction of all else.

It is not an easy thing to still the mind, however, there will be more times of stillness when we cease frantically attempting to "outguess" tomorrow. The best way to insure this form of stillness is to refuse to live in thoughts of yesterday and projections into tomorrow. Through the stillness that is NOW will come new ways to view the world that surrounds you. The ability to see purely will become activated. To see purely is to see from the single center. The single center exists as the eye of a hurricane, quiet within the storm. There is no conscious thought here, there is trust instead. Trust that which we do receives guidance from a higher nature that lives within us.

"LIFE CYCLE"

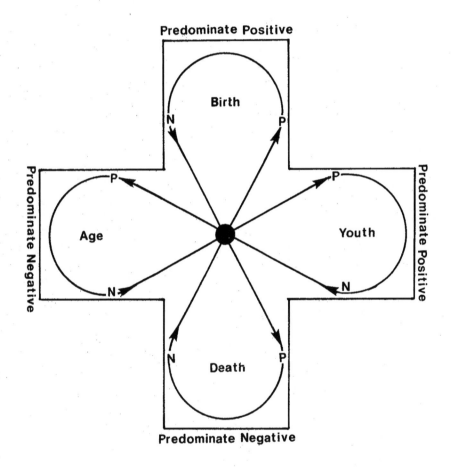

172

OPPOSITES OF THE "LIFE CYCLE" CHART

BIRTH

POSITIVE - NEGATIVE CONTENT

Birth contains the element of newness coupled with the potential of death.

DEATH

POSITIVE - NEGATIVE CONTENT

Death spells the end of the familiar, as well as containing the element of newness of the unfamiliar. Hope of the prospect of an after life resides in the despair of contemplating death.

YOUTH

POSITIVE - NEGATIVE CONTENT

The obvious bloom of youth is a joy to observe. The painful adjustments to life that the young must make injects a negative aspect into the prospect of youth.

AGE

POSITIVE - NEGATIVE CONTENT

Age is a sceptor of death. The aging body, a painful condition to experience physically, is psychologically overshadowed as death becomes an eminent fact that must be faced. With age, however, comes an acceptance unknown to youth, an inner agreement that this physical form shall perish. It is said that old people tend to turn to thoughts of religion. Some say this is because they are unable to do the things that occupied them in the days of their youth. This is true, as a matter of nature, but this fact does not negate the truths of one's religion that suggest a continuing of life in another realm of consciousness.

CENTER

The Center of this chart conveys an observance of all stages of life, with the recognition that any one of these stages is not necessarily superior to another. Each stage contains some "good" and some "bad" aspects. A central agreement to acknowledge these particular stages of life, as one experiences them, brings to consciousness, a focused awareness that one is the manifestation of the "essence" of life in all of its stages.

PROJECTING DEATH

The thought of death is a constant companion to life. A great deal of speculation as to whether there is life after death is indulged in, as if the death aspect contains the answer to the mystery of life. The question arises from a conscious life standpoint, the answer must therefore lie in life itself, for from a personal point of "present state of awareness" can come our only reality.

The self imagined experience that is "death" to us is mentally lived many times by each person. We have no knowledge of the death experience so we can only conjecture.

"A coward dies a thousand deaths, a brave man only one".*

It is safe to say that all people die a thousand deaths, and this imagery is not limited to cowards. From the time we learn that we must die, we wonder what it will be like. We know that it will be different from anything we have known and that all things familiar to us will no longer exist. It is this fear of the unknown that gives death its fascinating hold on our minds.

We may choose to "die" as many or as few times as we wish by realizing that this is nothing but imagination allowed to run amuck, with no possible solution or conclusion to this mental "fearing of the unknown". The spiritual consciousness is eternal, each person is a part of that spiritual consciousness. If you keep your attention on the NOW moment you shall have everlasting life.

LOSS OF ANOTHER

The same principles that apply to self death speculation are applicable as well to "other" death speculation. We suffer needlessly in our sorrow for others, as we can have no true knowledge of the death experience. The painful "imaginings" on our part of what the other may have experienced have no reality other than we give to them. Perpetuating these self inflicted hurts by reliving the imagined experience of another is a self assumed, empty burden.

Termination of a close relationship regardless of the cause results in disorientation due to lack of self identification: "I became a certain thing to myself through this association, now this person is no longer here to tell me

174

* William Shakespeare

who I am". Grief is a natural emotion. In a mentally healthy person the change is gradually accepted, after a period of mourning and adjustment and the self image is reconstructed minus this particular source of self identification. This reorientation occurs through the Centered self. It is a healing. Denial of the Centered self results in continuing depression and loss of interest in life. To insist on any set self identification is to court self destruction.

WORRY REGARDING OTHERS

On the surface this seems to be a kind thing to do, but is in actuality a mental projection stemming from some insecurity in self. The self image is reliant upon another for support in some manner. If the self image identifies as a wife/mother, husband/father, etc., and something should happen to remove the source of self identification, the self image would become disoriented. It is this fear for self, that is the cause of emotional frenzy concerning another's safety when there is no factual basis for this concern, as is the case most of the time when one "worrys". Concern for another is not the same as worry for another. Vivid imaginings regarding ill fate to another cannot in any manner bring anything of worth to them. When you feel concern for another, send love. Love is free. To worry regarding another destroys your peace of mind while bolstering a false self image of dependency. Each person is a child of God. Each is destined to fulfill his particular reason in life and as such is in no danger.

YOUTH - AGE

Youth is fleeing. To experience disorientation due to the physical changes of aging is the fate of all people. The shock of seeing lines and gray hair reflected in one's mirror is indicative of the relentless battle of the false self image to resist change; to identify only with the self image he was familiar with in his youth. When one is able to view his changing reflection with full acceptance of the lines and gray hair, he is alive to the moment and the vitality that is life will course through his body with the full vigor that he experienced in his youthful years. To live any other way is to live on only as a mourner for his own lost dead youth. Youth does not have a corner on the joys of life. We must become fully oriented to the present moment. To accept ourselves as we are NOW is to be alive NOW. One cannot buy youth in a beauty parlor, he can only create for himself the illusion of youth. How much simpler to see that age is also an illusion of the false self image.

HEALTH

People are visiting doctors like never before in history. We are experiencing a mass health-illness phobia. The stresses of living in today's world take their toll upon the physical body. It must be remembered that these stresses are a product of the uncontrolled mind. Situations are not distressing, emotional reactions are distressing. The majority of visits to doctors are simply pleas for reassurance that all is well. We have become a doctor oriented society. If people only went to doctors when they are really in need of medical care, the doctors would have to work at other jobs to suppliment their income. When one has gained control of his own mind and ceases to promote distressing reactions to outer conditions, his body will be allowed to function in a normal manner. The body is constantly attempting to repair itself for the will to survive is contained within each cell structure.

There are more radical health problems that arise when one has been subjected to an accident or illness that has altered his self image. The first emotional reaction is depression. He longs for the loss of his old self. Sudden loss of the self image in any manner is overwhelming. The courage of many people as they become reoriented to a new self image is the subject of many heartwarming stories. A person reading the accounts of rehabilitation in the face of almost overwhelming odds must ask himself if he would be capable of such courage. The answer is "yes". The Center of self is life, a force so strong as to conquer anything it must in order to survive. Unfortunately, this source of strength is rarely tapped except in emergency situations. It exists in everyone.

PROJECTING THE IMAGE IN THE MIRROR

Much of a person's sense of self worth is based on his own perception of his physical appearance. Here too, he receives approval and disapproval from within. This has little or nothing to do with the opinions of others. Some people are Narcissistic regarding their own physical appearance. The opposite extreme is complete rejection of one's own physical appearance wherein one insists he is ugly. No amount of outside influence will change the way a person basically views his physical self. This is borne out in cases of reconstructive surgery that bring about physical beauty but the patient still insists that he is "ugly".

The state of mind must change before the perception of the physical self image can change. Plastic surgery of any kind is not necessary when a person truly accepts himself. There is nothing wrong in taking care of one's personal appearance even to the point of corrective surgery, if the patient is not expecting this "change" in himself to cause him to be more acceptable to others.

The outer physical appearance does not have much in common with one's beliefs regarding his appearance, as he has decided to like or dislike certain aspects of himself. One's physical "reality" begins in the mind and extends through self projection. No matter how one may appear to others, he carries this mental picture of himself which becomes for all intents and purposes his physical appearance reality.

As no two people view any one person in the same light, you have only one steady reference point and that is your own. When one accepts his physical self and feels good about himself, he will relax and accept his physical appearance whatever it may be. This form of self acceptance has a bonus effect as the face is lighted up from within reflecting the inner enjoyment of life. No amount of facial beauty can compare to a smile of open friendliness to another person.

When society's standards of beauty are accepted by one's self then he will constantly be comparing himself to potential rivals. Feelings of superiority and inferiority will cloud your pure vision regarding your self worth as based on physical appearance. The human being is the only form of life that questions its own value. All other forms of life simply "are" The human mentally determines his value by comparing himself with other humans. He then torments himself with these comparisons. As the highest form of intelligence known to life, it does not appear that we are making ultimate use of the intelligence that has been bestowed on us.

PROJECTING ROLES

CHRONOLOGICAL AGE - EMOTIONAL AGE

The years do not necessarily bring with them emotional maturity. There is no one magic age in which one suddenly finds himself "grown up" emotionally. Many and even most, of the adjustment problems discussed in this book have been allocated to the callowness of youth. Society assumes that when one is no longer young he does not experience these self conflicts, and projects "maturity" upon those who physically appear to be so. This is unfortunate, for when one assumes that he is "grown up" emotionally, he will discontinue any effort to learn more of this aspect of himself.

There is no generation gap existing in the emotional ages of most parents and children. Each "stage" of life is entirely new to the individual who finds himself in unfamiliar territory. At the same time the child is learning, so is the parent. Unfortunately the parent may believe he already knows, and while he has learned a great many things that the child has yet to learn, these things that "he knows" have to do with exterior things. The average parent becomes "emotionally upset" when his child refuses to heed his sage advice. This emotional reaction of the parent indicates his own emotional imaturity, for a simple fact of life, is that each person must experience life for himself in order to gain awareness of the truth in each thing. One tends to forget his own youthful battles with the "older generation", and as he grows older he assumes the role his elders claimed and laments the "younger generation". This cycle has been perpetuated from the beginning of time as is obvious to anyone who cares to see.

To some degree, we may not care to see, for to admit that this is true, we must admit that we have not "grown up", we have only grown older. This self admission contains release from burdens that one places on himself in the effort to be an all knowing, perfect parent. We have more in common with our children than we may know, for knowledge of the emotional aspect of the human being is in it's infancy. In this area we are all as babes.

PROJECTING ROLES

Others are viewed through self comprehension, consequently, no one person is viewed in the same way by any two people. Until one has proven otherwise, and maybe even beyond this point, our views of others are highly subjective, i.e. if one is of a trusting nature he tends to trust others, if one is of a suspicious nature, he believes all people are suspicious. If you have ever wondered what you did that caused another to dislike you, you may have done nothing, he may have transferred a self conflict to you.

To have faith in a person, or the general population as a whole; "faith in humanity", is to believe that people will perform according to what you believe to be the right way to perform. This will not always be so, for they will perform in the way they wish to, or must, according to the circumstances. When one expects others to live up to his ideals and they do not, he feels that others have "let him down". When one ceases to place his faith in "humanity" he is releasing himself from the burden of judgment of humanity and finds faith in his own strength to be more determining and reliable to bring about his own desired results.

Kahil Gibran expresses the human desire to own and influence others in this statement from the Prophet:

> Your children are not your children,
> They are the sons and daughters
> Of life's longing for itself.
> They come through you but not from you,
> And though they are with you yet
> They belong not to you. *

This releasing of others can and should be extended to include all of one's family, friends, acquaintances, in fact all of humanity. The tendency to project people into roles that please us as if we owned them, should cease. Each person belongs to himself, to be that expression of life that he has chosen to be.

LET GO.......

*Kahil Gibran, the Prophet (New York; Alfred A. Knopf Publisher pg. 17.

FOUR RULES OF RELEASE

1. Do not place people in roles that please you and become emotionally upset if they do not "play the part". Do not withold your love as punishment.

2. Do not assume that others owe it to you to please you, regardless of the circumstances and become angry at "their" self centeredness.

3. Do not be "proud" of another's accomplishments, be happy for them in their success. To say "I am proud of you" indicates an approval based situation, it indicates an opposite reaction would be forthcoming had they failed. To say, "I am happy for you in your success" allows freedom from the burden of gaining another's approval. This allows the other person to feel whole and unjudged.

4. Do not cling and demand that others provide support, for each should be self supporting and respective of another's ability to be this self contained individual also.

NEED

We experience many adverse emotional reactions because we NEED others to agree with us, to love us, to strengthen us, to reflect us favorably, etc. Most adverse emotional experiences are the result of some NEED of support from the outer world. As long as we NEED from others, we shall only anguish, unfulfilled. Fulfillment must come from the realization of one's own natural state of wholeness. This is not in order to isolate one's self from others, just the opposite, it is to he can interact with others in a self supporting manner, so that he has something of value to give others. All people have something of value to give, but what they have to give another from a whole state of self is a releasing of the other person from the burden of support in a relationship. They have the ability to allow another to be himself, make mistakes, etc., while remaining acceptable as a person. It is loving others while needing nothing

nothing from them. It is not identifying self in another person. It is knowing you are complete within yourself when love is not forthcoming from another.

Whatever problems you experience of a lonely nature begin within yourself. You will be lonely until you have recognized your own natural state of wholeness. No other person can provide this reassurance for you, nor should you expect them to. To some extent this confusion lies in the male-female differences. One feels that one of the opposite sex is necessary in his life to make him complete. This male-female difference is only one more example of opposites existing in all things and one cannot look to any one set of opposites and expect to solve all of his conflicts through resolving this one aspect of life.

Each person searches for his perfect mate. He carries a mental picture of this person in his mind. When he meets someone who appears to have all of the qualities for which he has been searching, he "falls in love" with that person. One is already "in love" with his illusion of the perfect mate and he places his illusion upon a real live person as the object of his search. He is convinced he shall be happy ever after with this union conceived in heaven.

When this relationship progresses to include day to day intimacy the illusion begins to fade, this person appears to be other than he/she originally appeared to be. The common complaint that the other person changed or misrepresented himself is behind many broken relationships. One must be willing to "fall out of love" with his projected illusion, before he can see clearly enough to choose a mate for a lasting relationship built on total acceptance of the other person as they really are. Each person, really is: human, with human faults. Good relationships are not conceived in heaven, they are conceived on earthly acceptance of human nature.

PROJECTED SENSITIVITY FIELD

You silently tell others how to view you. This is non verbal communication. Your self image "aura" is received by others even before you speak. This form of communication speaks louder than words. Words are often misunderstood. The subtle exchanges of combined sensitivity fields are never misunderstood. Entire exchanges of personal interaction take place simultaneously with the spoken language. This is accomplished partly through body language and tones of voice, however, to rely on these surface interpretations alone is not sufficient.

Mental telepathy of this type is actually a basic part of human makeup. These are not word messages but vibrations from the sensitivity field that surrounds each person. This sensitivity field preceeded the sophisticated method of communication. Language is subject to personal interpretation on a conscious mental level, the sensitivity field is not. Animals use this sensitivity field exclusively for intercommunication. It is not likely that they ever misunderstand each other as the sensitivity confrontation takes place.* **see note pg 139**

Many times the spoken word may contradict vibrations (hunches) received. If these two things do not coincide, heed the vibrations. Do not undermine yourself in a relationship that can only bring unhappiness to you, for when you receive sensitivity warnings that all is not well with a relationship, you can only be creating for yourself an unhappy reality by pursuing it against your inner heedings. If approval (acceptance) is not forthcoming from another, do not resort to manipulation to force this acceptance of yourself. In the first place you do not need it and in the second place you will only ultimately bring unhappiness to yourself.

You will not please all people, accept this as a matter of course and encourage close associations only where you are accepted as you are. If you must take on any particular adverse feeling toward yourself to maintain any relationship, see that it is not worth the price and leave that person to himself.

TO THINE OWN SELF BE TRUE*

"Do unto others as you would have them do unto you".*

One may think to himself: "I did treat that person as I would like to be treated and yet he did not reciprocate. What sense does this saying make?"

, Author Unknown
* Matt. 7.12

This precept does not state that the reverse is true and that we will or should do unto others as they have done to us. The inclination to "get even" with another person for ill treatment requires that you betray your own values of what is proper conduct.

We must remain true to ourselves or we have nothing. To do unto others as you would have them do unto you is a demonstration of remaining true to yourself regardless of the behaviour of others.

*Note: The sensitivity field is not mental telepathy per se as random thoughts are not meant to be observed by another. We are sometimes aware of fleeting thoughts that we ourselves would not entertain. Human mental privacy is assured, as it must be. Current explorations of the powers of the mind indicate latent possibilities existing in fields such as directed mental telepathy, psychonesis, etc. These explorations offer exciting possibilities, but these powers of the mind cannot solve the emotional problems faced by humanity. The mental energies should first be turned to self understanding, as our mental powers can only be weakened by exhausting emotional conflicts within the self.

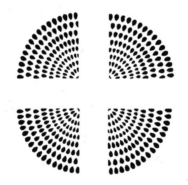

PERCEPTION

PERCEPTION

Projection is often mistaken for perception. Projection of this type has a very strong influence on one's personal experience of reality. As a part of oneself is projected into each experience we generally see what we want to see.

While one must be aware that he is projecting his thoughts into the words and actions of others, he must also be aware that the other person is really there. Another person is not just a cloudy figment of one's imagination, he is just as real as you are.

Each person functions mentally as:

OBSERVER
SENSOR
INTERPRETOR
PROJECTOR

We do not perceive of each other's version of reality, but we do interact through this area of shadow reality that exists between us.

SHADOW REALITY

The fact that each person interprets situations differently is not as important as the fact that each person believes that others see things the same way he does and is being deliberately obstinate. It is from this confusion that much anger, and feelings of self pity arise. If each person was aware that they are not in total communication with another, and took this fact into consideration upon encounter with another, they would tend to be more tolerant of themselves and the other person.

Sincere attempts are made to communicate our position to another with the use of words. Words are simply inadequate due to unique interpretation by each person. The area of shadow reality is indeed nebulous because it conveys neither person's sincere feelings regarding any subject. Each situation consists of a triangle: the way I see it, the way you see it, and the way it is.

INTERACTION WITH OTHERS

AREA OF SHADOW REALITY

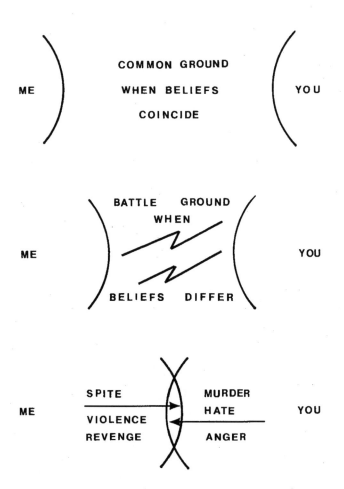

ME)   COMMON GROUND
        WHEN BELIEFS
        COINCIDE   (YOU

ME)   BATTLE GROUND
           WHEN
        BELIEFS DIFFER (YOU

ME   SPITE   MURDER   YOU
     VIOLENCE   HATE
     REVENGE   ANGER

When Beliefs Collide

The above illustrations demonstrate attempts to solve problems through relationships with others without first resolving conflicts within self. Results are infringement of each others rightful space. Each person is one half of the battle.

SECTION FOUR

The

Centered

Self

INTEGRATION

SELF APPROVAL

We are taught, at a very young age, that to be a "good", "superior", "loving", giving", person will bring about public approval and with it the longed for reward in the form of personal happiness. Parents unknowingly, participate in perpetuating this fallacy by rewarding their children for exemplorary behaviour through bestowing approval upon their attractive, intelligent, good children, words of praise and love. They also bestow upon their children, disapproval, judgment, and denial of "love", if the child fails to act as the parent believes they should. Reward and punishment are the rules of emotional orientation.

When a child becomes an adult, parents are no longer the final determiners of our value and society as a whole becomes our judge and jury. The "laws" of society must be conformed to if one is to remain a "free" individual, this is accomplished by the majority of people, however, this majority is an unhappy lot, searching for their "reward".

While one receives payment for services rendered, the reassurance that one is "good" is not forthcoming from society, except to a very favored few. This recognition comes about in the form of "fame". To be rich and famous would fulfill the "child" in self, this is true, but would not fulfill the adult in self. If one could see that his most basic need of reassurance came about as a product of "society's training" that resulted in a dependence upon outer conditions supplying self support, the need to amass money or to receive public adulation would disolve from the emotional system. Physical luxuries and approval from others are certainly very nice things to have, however, if one would still retain his happiness if they were all to disappear, he knows that he has "grown up" and no longer needs these "rewards" to supply an emotional need of a misguided child.

SELF STRENGTH

When a person has exhausted all other possible sources of strength in times of stress, in final desperation he finds a new source of strength existing within himself. This type of occurrence is born out in tales of people who experience intense suffering reporting a "religious" experience that provided a renewed sense of strength. This may be misconstrued as one being "worthy" of God's revelation through suffering. There are many kinds of suffering, some of which are not visible to anyone other than the sufferer. When one has suffered enough he gives his suffering over to a deeper strength to handle. This is known as giving your problems to God. As long as one believes he can handle a problem through thought process alone he will not turn to the "Centered" strength. Regardless of one's personal religious beliefs, that may or may not encompass a "God" concept, there is no denying the added strength that one is capable of when he experiences "integration" of the separated (weakening) self aspects that evolve from believing that he knows all of the answers.

NEWNESS

In an effort aimed at "orientation" one tends to mentally-visually fill in missing pieces of each thing observed, in order to feel comfortable with a total picture of his surroundings. This mental-visual action provides "instant" orientation and brings with it the comfortable feeling that one knows what is occurring.

It also brings with it, a dulling of the senses, for when we believe we know what is occurring we do not look further. The subconscious mind of the adult is full of missing pieces (preconceived ideas) that he projects onto the "present state of awareness" according to current need, and then mistakenly believes he is living NOW but is only experiencing reruns of previously drawn conclusions.

The pure Center is a state of present awareness that is not only free of preconceived ideas derived from emotional experiences of the past, but is also a state of mind that does not demand that each observation necessarily bring about a hard "conclusion" that supports material orientation. A child lives from this pure Center: remember the excitment of

194

discovery that you experienced as a child? This pure state is eventually forfeited as the child grows and joins the unseeing world of the adult in which one lives almost totally from his own projections onto the world.

It is necessary to acknowledge the need for "structure" in the world of matter, for we need these structures to lend form to our existance. If one attempts to obsolve all structure from his life, he ceases to progress as an actively participating member of society and may spend his life "contemplating the universe." It is necessary to strive for balance between the actual "living" of life, and the search for a meaning to life. To become lost to the active participation of the very things that we search for a meaning to, becomes a ludricrous proposition.
This balance can be achieved by reserving analytical observations to the areas of life for which they are meant. The balance that we achieved in the process of learning to walk is descriptive of the very necessary observation of "structure" that must be recognized. We "over" structure our existances when we attempt to provide instant orientation to things that not only do not require absolute structure, but must be left to the moment if one is to experience life with "newness".

ACCEPTANCE

The acceptance of things one cannot change is not the same as defeatism. It is a peaceful acknowledgment that some things will be as opposed to the way one would prefer them to be. Through this peaceful acceptance one retains absolute emotional control as the personal world of his own mind remains calm.

It may seem that one is only "fooling" himself when he chooses to keep smiling when things are going badly. Because one is "aware" of the conditions that do not spell out ultimate happiness does not mean that these conditions are more self determining than the things that are at the same time, going right. What one "focuses" his attention on results in his emotional reality, which is after all, the only reality we know. We have all seen people who are always smiling, regardless of their circumstances. We may secretly feel they are not too bright. Can't they see what a mess the world is in? They see it all right, they have just chosen not to focus on it.

THE CENTERED SELF

"Through my beliefs, I became me, a unique spark of the universal consciousness. I stand "Centered" between the sea of opposites and have chosen 'this over that' as guide lines for my existance. These guide lines serve to aid me in my search for individulism. I see these beliefs as something apart from my "Centered" self, and do not give them the power to stifle my growth as a person, for it is only when I mistake these beliefs for 'myself' that I become outraged if anyone threatens to undermine these beliefs. In my state of self approval, I leave you to your peace. In your state of self approval, you leave me to mine. In this state of mutual agreement we can work together for the betterment of humanity."

There is no situation outside of actual physical attack that does not respond for the better to a change from inside the self that causes one to view exterior conditions in a more favorable light. (Change from within the self will also do much to ward off physical attacks). Situations, in themselves, are not the problem. Most relationships become intolerable when two people are approaching one another with preset attitudes that stem from feelings of self pity and angry self defense. You cannot change another person but you can claim your own liberation without physically moving away. It is possible another person will respond for the better to the change in you. It is also possible that he will not. Define for yourself the boundries that leave you feeling "whole" and do not tolerate infringment on these boundries. This is done mentally, not emotionally. Firmly claim your own "space" and allow the other person to be what he is. When he senses the resolvement in you, he has no choice but to take his inner battles elsewhere for airing.

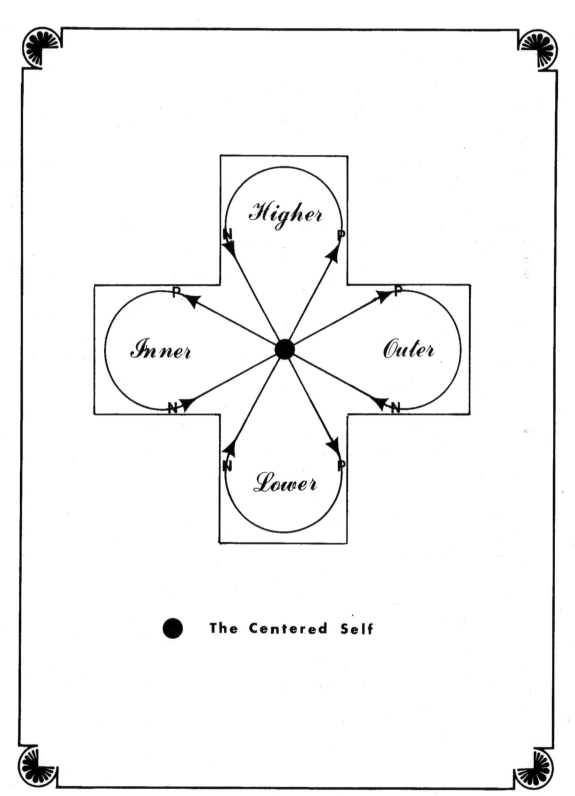

The Centered Self

You will observe the existance of confused people hell bent on destroying themselves and everything around them. Observation without condemnation or personal inner trumoil means that you have taken leave of this emotional roller coaster that says you must act as judge and jury of all things.

The other person is very much like you are. He has his hopes and dreams, his successes and failures. He has his right to believe as he wishes just as you do. It is not necessary that you agree on all things. It isn't even necessary that you agree on anything. For each of us has the right to be ourselves. If we respect another person's right to be himself and quietly reserve our own rights there will be little disagreement between us. When we each claim our own state of wholeness we will have very little to disagree on. The fearful state of being that demands too much from another is the cause of the majority of conflict between persons. The insistance that we receive approval from all people leads us to demand too much from one another.

Allow the other person to be himself. It is not necessary that we itemize and lable each person that we meet, as if it were necessary to take inventory and catalog each and every person for quick and easy reference. This may make life easier as far as "things" are concerned, but when we carry this mental action over to include people, we will miss a great deal of what each person has to offer as a live, changeable, human being. Try to keep an open mind when encountering another person. Listen to what they are trying to convey. Attempt to see that person as "new" with each meeting. You will never be bored with another's company when you do this. Boredom is a product of the self, not exterior conditions.

When we leave others to be themselves and recognize our problems as existing within ourselves, we will have a great deal of concentrated energy to direct toward self realization. For when we have assumed responsibility for ourselves we have gained control of ourselves. We can then expend our energies toward "being" that Quintessence of life that we were born to be.

It is entirely up to you to create your own happiness. Conscious contact with the pure Center puts one in a state of grace. The Center remains uneducated to the sophisticated ways of the human world and sees through the eyes of nature. There exists an uncanny beauty in each material thing when viewed without comparison that reveals the purpose of each thing as it exists complete within itself.

To remain in contact with this state of grace requires alert attention on your part. When you allow your peace to be disturbed through needless mind analyzation you become "separated" within yourself. A state of "wholeness" is always there waiting for you to return, as grace is a part of your human condition just as mental confusion is a part. Choose your emotional experience and work for it. Adverse conditions surround you daily, pure observation places them in proper proportion. Life is ordered. There exists no confusion in things, there is only confusion in the mind. Life exhibits a natural flow, an even pulsation of continuity. Quiet the mind and accept the existing order.

The pure Center does not demand security, it does not know of conflict. As long as we set our hearts on one particular circumstance as opposed to another, reserving our personal happiness for this happening only, we will be unhappy, constantly searching and never finding. Hopes and dreams are a part of human nature, we need to aspire to give meaning to our lives, but to reserve our happiness for the acquisition of the hope and dream is not to live at all. This one moment in time is all that I shall ever truly have and when viewed minus confusion, it is beautiful to be alive.

This Moment

This book is based on "visualizations" experienced by the author during meditation. The evolvement of this Mandala, over a four year period, served as a guide.

MANDALA

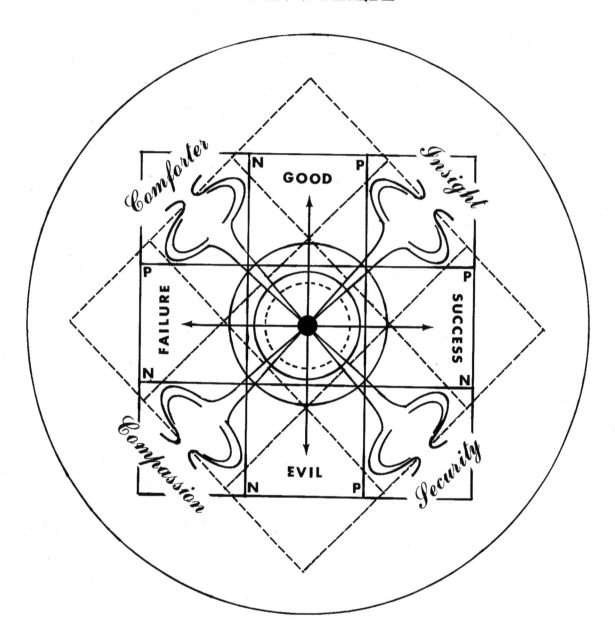

RECONCILIATION OF THE OPPOSITES